ADVANCE PRAISE

"Inspiring read on how science and spirituality can complement each other to enhance our experience on this planet."

—OZAN VAROL, BESTSELLING AUTHOR
OF *THINK LIKE A ROCKET SCIENTIST*

"Doug is one of the most passionate and intelligent seekers of our generation. For those who are on the same path, this book is a must-read. We all can learn a lot from his journey to speed up our own."

—KRISTEN ULMER, FORMER WORLD-CLASS
ATHLETE, AUTHOR OF *THE ART OF FEAR*

"Doug is one of the most enthusiastic magical thinkers I have ever known. Just being around him changes your frequency. Follow what he says, but, most importantly, just follow this guy. He will remind you why unicorns are real."

—BIET SIMKIN, SPIRITUAL TEACHER,
AUTHOR OF *DON'T JUST SIT THERE!*

HOLY SH!T WE'RE ALIVE

NOW WHAT?

DOUG CARTWRIGHT

LIONCREST
PUBLISHING

HOLY SH!T WE'RE ALIVE
Now What?

ISBN   978-1-5445-2120-6 *Hardcover*
          978-1-5445-2119-0 *Paperback*
          978-1-5445-2118-3 *Ebook*

Dedicated to my father, who I wish could read this; my lovely mother; my inspiring siblings; and all the incredible friends who supported me along my journey.

CONTENTS

FOREWORD

BY KELSEY WELLS,
GLOBAL FITNESS STAR AND
SELF-EMPOWERMENT ADVOCATE

One ordinary Saturday afternoon, Doug Cartwright—the brother-in-law to my good friend and a vague acquaintance of mine—strolled up to me at the gym, enveloped in a confidence and joy that made no sense whatsoever. With fervency, he shared with me a profound experience he'd had, simply "because [he] knew [I] needed to know." I laughed and left feeling an abundance of love for him and with the distinct thought that, although I should think he'd gone batshit crazy, instead I knew he was simply, truly alive. I would soon find out that, the things he'd shared that day, I did, indeed, need to know.

That is what happens when we live and share our truth unashamedly—vulnerability breeds connection, and connection breeds healing.

Because *truth* has a feeling.

That ordinary Saturday afternoon was right on time, and soon, Doug Cartwright became a very close friend of mine. Witnessing Doug awaken to his truth (while awakening to my own) through the years since has been an absolute gift; one best summarized as a collection of touchpoints, encouragement, and conversations—*always* right on time and always leaving me feeling/thinking, *HOLY SHIT, WE ARE ALIVE!?!!! Holy shit, we're alive.*

Doug birthed this book into this world because he was meant to.

Whatever it is that made you pick up this book? Know you were meant to.

Congratulations! You are now holding in your hand one incredibly and brilliantly alive human's raw and honest truth.

Pay attention to the pieces and chapters that speak to *you*— because, make no mistake, they are meant to.

INTRODUCTION

This is my story—the psychedelically sparked spiritual journey of an ex-Mormon millionaire. If that already sounds kind of crazy, you have no idea how wild it's about to get. I definitely didn't when I first started down this path.

If you picked this up thinking it was just another ~~boring~~ enlightening self-help book, you're in the wrong place. I've read so many of them and have nothing earth-shattering or groundbreaking to add to the genre. At this point, I end up putting those books back on the shelf after two paragraphs anyway because they all sound the same.

It's also not really a memoir, even though it follows my travels around both the globe and the woo-woo world, trying anything and everything to calm the angst and depression I felt on the inside despite seemingly "having it all" on the outside. I did astrology. Biofeedback. Biohacking. Burning Man. Cryotherapy. Crystals. Ecstatic dancing. EMDR. Energy work. Flotation tanks. Flow camp. Holotropic breathwork. Intermittent fasting. Meditation. Healing psychedelic plant medicine ceremonies with 5-MeO-DMT, ayahuasca, MDMA, and psilocybin. Psychics. Reiki. Shamans. Silent retreats. Sound Baths. Spiritual coaching. Sweat lodges. Wim Hoff Method. Yoga (so much yoga!), at home and in Bali. These provided some major, life-altering realizations—although the biggest ones were actually jump-started by the more mundane and universal experience of heartbreak—that helped lead me to the authentic, happy, fulfilled place I'm in now, but no single thing was a magic bullet.

See, for way too long, I was wrapped up in my "fat kid" self-image that hadn't been true for years. My dad died when I was in my early twenties, and I shoved all that grief down and didn't deal with it until it came back and slapped me in the face. I tried to be perfect at the religion I was raised in, nearly drowned in the shame of not being perfect, and finally left the church knowing imperfection is what being human is all about. I made a ton of money (and spent a ton of money) at a job where they called me "The King," but that didn't stop me from having suicidal thoughts and wanting a Corvette speeding by to kill me, so I wouldn't have to do it myself. I basically had to lose everything I ever thought defined me before I could redefine myself and my life on my own terms. It was hard, and it was painful, but nothing has ever been more worth it.

Whatever your story is, I'm guessing you wouldn't be reading this book unless you were carrying around a similar seed of unhappiness that doesn't seem to go away no matter what you do. Maybe you've even dabbled in meditation, mindfulness seminars, and millionaire masterminds trying to get rid of it. If you feel like any of that is helping, by all means, keep doing it. But after everything I tried, I know one thing for sure: if you still don't feel healed, alive, and excited about your existence, it's time to give something new a shot.

As author and astrophysicist Neil deGrasse Tyson once said, "It's easier to be told by others what to think and believe than it is to think for yourself." So, I'm definitely not here to tell you what to think. Instead, I want to offer you some tools that can help you think for yourself and let go of the same old ideas that got you here in the first place. Hopefully, my story will inspire you to make changes of your own and spark a new zest for loving, enjoying, and fully participating in your life.

I don't claim to be an industry know-it-all. I'm a certified meditation teacher, but I'm not a therapist with a bunch of fancy degrees hanging on my wall (TBH, I was a finance major). So, what makes me qualified to teach you how to live more deeply and enjoy life more fully? Because I have been in the cave.

I've squandered the money, dealt with the body shame, felt the guilt, lost the person closest to me, suffered the sexual abuse, went through the religious existential crisis, had my heart broken, contemplated suicide, and been on the verge of a public freak-out. If you find yourself in your own cave— no matter what the reason—this book provides a flashlight and map out of there. It will help you emerge from the darkness, ditch those anxious thoughts, and foster a calm mindset for a change.

In sharing my story, I hope to leave you with a few insights that will help quiet the voice inside your head, ease your constant restlessness and angst, and uncover the subconscious stories that may be secretly guiding your life. I want to give you the opportunity to find a new path and the courage and permission to be your truest, most authentic self. I want to help you realize where you are right now is perfect—you have special gifts no one else has, and you can share them with the world.

When you're done reading this book, my biggest wish is that you'll love being you like I finally love being me, and life won't bother you anymore because it's a beautiful experience to be had, not a problem to solve. The end goal is that you'll be so full of love you'll have no choice but to share it with others and help them feel the same way.

You up for it? Let's go.

CHAPTER ONE

WE SHOULDN'T EVEN BE ALIVE

Back when I was still trying to claw my way to the top of the corporate ladder, stuck on the "keeping up with the Joneses" hamster wheel, I wondered how some people seemed to have life all figured out. They were truly leveled up: inspiring, joyful, authentic, easy to be around and talk to. It seemed like they were human magnets for happiness, fun, and personal growth.

I thought they were in on a giant secret no one was telling me. Why were they so happy, and why was I still wallowing? I had accomplished everything I was "supposed" to by that point, but it still seemed like I was missing a key piece of information for enjoying life. I was always asking myself, "What do they know that I don't?"

After spending over $100,000 and multiple years of my life trying to find the answer, I finally figured it out: the secret to life is there is no secret. A life centered in self-love is all we truly need to enjoy the experiences we've been given here. We are all part of a larger whole, and loving ourselves is the basis for genuinely being able to love and help others.

Life is beautiful. Everything is exactly how it's supposed to be. There is no finish line we need to get to before we can finally enjoy ourselves and help out the people we care about. We can just do it now.

Sound too simple to be true? It's not, really. I'll explain how I got to this place as we go along and give you the tools to help you get there too. For now, though, let's start here: It's easy to be grateful for everything I have these days when I know from a cosmic perspective *we shouldn't even be alive.*

For real. The odds are so stacked against us. The chances of you sitting here, reading this book, right now? Basically 0 percent. And yet, here we are.

WHAT'S *REALLY* HAPPENING HERE?

Knowing we are a literal speck in the universe filled me with awe and wonder but also left me with a lot of questions. Like, how did all this get here? What is actually going on right now? This moment right in front of me—where was it created? And who, if anyone, put all this matter together?

I turned to science for answers and learned some absolutely mind-bending statistics. For instance: as you read this, we're literally on a giant rock, orbiting a star, hurtling sixty thousand miles an hour through space. Think about that for a second. Right now—this very moment—we're on a massive boulder zooming through the cosmos. We're actually riding on a supersized stone spaceship.

Or how about this? In our own galaxy, there are roughly one hundred billion other planets and more than three hundred billion other stars doing the same thing. Beyond the Milky Way, another estimated two trillion galaxies in this universe, each with their own millions of planets and billions of stars.

Let's do the math here. With an estimated two trillion galaxies and one hundred billion planets per galaxy, that means there could be two hundred quintillion (that's a 2 followed by twenty-three zeros!) other possible planets. A figure that large is essentially incomprehensible. There's no way we can think we're the center of the universe given numbers like that.

My Brain Hurts Now!

I still sometimes look at photos of Earth taken from space to remind me of my ayahuasca experience. If I cover our planet with my thumb, I've come to realize it doesn't change the picture much at all. The earth could explode, and every person, idea, piece of art, music, emotion, and experience that ever existed would disappear—and it wouldn't even make a single dent in the universe. The cosmos would go on like we'd never existed in the first place.

Poof! Our planet, humanity—gone forever. Just like that. No one would ever know we'd been here at all.

Mind officially blown!!!!.

FROM ATOMS TO ALL OF US

Remember in junior high when we learned everything is made up of atoms? Once I realized what a tiny nothing we are in terms of the entire universe, I started wondering, *Where did all those atoms come from? How is it possible—on this one little planet flying around space with an almost unfathomable number of others—that there's life? How do we even exist in the first place?*

The Spark Notes version of it goes like this:

- 13.8 billion years ago, the entire universe fit into the size of an atom. Scientists can trace the beginning of its existence because light has a constant speed, which can be seen using our most high-powered telescopes.
- It suddenly exploded—the Big Bang—and white plasma went everywhere.

- The electrons in the plasma started to attract protons using gravity.
- After expanding for approximately three hundred thousand to five hundred thousand years, those atoms cooled down, and the protons and neutrons came together to create hydrogen. For a long time, there was nothing but hydrogen atoms in the universe.
- Hydrogen atoms eventually pulled together using gravity, creating helium.
- This created stars—the first light!
- When the core of helium in those stars ran out of hydrogen to burn, they became red giant stars.
- When there was nothing left but helium mass in red giant stars, they morphed into white dwarf stars.
- The leftover helium in white dwarf stars fused into carbon—the same carbon we are made of: our DNA, bones, skin, and teeth.
- Carbon atoms created oxygen and lithium, then iron.
- This eventually created a supernova and the most spectacular explosion, the power of which crushed the iron core until it fused and created a nucleolar mass. (Fun fact: every piece of gold was created in this explosion, so you've actually seen and touched the fallout of a supernova!)
- As a result of this process, all 118 elements in the periodic table were created.
- Gravity pulled all the elements together, and voilà, planet earth was formed.

The most amazing part about it? None of this in any way contradicts the existence of God (or any other supreme being you put your faith into). It's not an either/or conundrum. If a creator did all of this, the Big Bang is the tool they used. The question isn't, *Did the Big Bang happen or not?* It's, *Who (if anything) was the intelligence behind the Big Bang?*

Clearly, us humans still don't know that answer. The only thing we know for sure is everything had to happen the exact, specific way it happened. It all had to go perfectly, or none of this would be here. None of *us* would be here. The odds of even being alive are four trillion to one.

So, the next time you're feeling anxious because there's a ten-minute line in Starbucks, remember the simple fact that there *is* a Starbucks, you have a giant piece of metal with four wheels that gets you around town, and you can place your order on a handheld rectangular device that can search for and locate any piece of information you want is absolutely insane.

We already hit the lottery just by being born.

THE REST IS A MYSTERY

But even though we've figured out the mind-boggling complexities of how life on Earth began, we still don't know very much about the universe as a whole. We've only gotten as far as identifying 5 percent of its matter, which is made up of things we know: stars, planets, gas, everything here on Earth (all of which are the result of the Big Bang). The other 95 percent is a complete mystery.

We call that mystery *dark matter* and *dark energy.* We can measure it because it affects gravity, but we still don't know what it is. We don't know what it's made of. We don't know how it's made. We don't know what it's doing. Think about that one: even the most brilliant scientists on Earth have no idea what's going on with it.

To give you an idea of how vast and vacant the universe is, consider this: if I was holding a photon—aka, a beam of light—and let it go, it would travel around the earth seven and a half times in one second. Pretty fast, right? But at that same rate of speed, it would take us four and a half years just to get the next nearest star—and that four-and-a-half-year trip would be through absolutely nothing. Just black, empty space.

Think of how many stars we see at night. *So many.* Still, it's mostly emptiness between those fireballs of light. There isn't much happening out there as far as we know. But for whatever reason, we got dropped on this beautiful planet where there's *so much* going on. How is that even possible?

It's totally weird, but it gets even weirder.

Since humans can only see 0.0035 percent of the electromagnetic spectrum, an entire universe of things that we're blind to might be hiding among all that dark matter. We, as humans, have limited receptors. Animals without conical photoreceptors don't even see color, but people see rainbows as light molecules hit our eyes. It could be a similar situation. We just don't know.

Another example: while babies get made inside us, we have no idea how to actually "make" babies. I'm serious! Do we have any clue where the intelligence to make lungs, eyeballs, and spinal fluid all sync up, so they work together, properly originated? Or how consciousness actually gets into us? Not even an inkling. The best we can say at the moment is the same forces that created the universe created us.

Our DNA is 99 percent the same as a chimpanzee's, but in that 1-percent difference is a massive gap of intelligence. A chimp can't go to college, pick up a pizza, or call an Uber to get to a basketball game at 7:00. The smartest ones can maybe put boxes on top of one another and count to ten.

So, what would happen if—given the vastness of the universe and the probability that other life exists—we met a species that was 1 percent smarter than us? How much would they know that we don't? They'd likely think our most brilliant thought leadership was pretty basic and limited. Our abilities would be the equivalent of stacking boxes and counting to ten compared to theirs.

We're a self-proclaimed intelligent species, but it's much more likely we are an extremely *unintelligent* species compared to whatever or whoever runs this universal show. Yet, despite our giant gaps in knowledge, the evolution of the human mind is still staggering. Ten thousand years ago, dolphins—arguably the smartest animals on the planet— were doing the same things they are today. They lived in the ocean then; they live in the ocean now. But we lived in caves back then, and now, we've figured out how to go to Mars, engineer cars that drive themselves, and create technology, so we can talk face-to-face with anyone, any- where, anytime using our phones and computers. So, not only are we incredibly lucky to just be here, but we have an opportunity to use these brilliant minds to learn, grow, and evolve.

As for the rest? It's a beautiful enigma. (At least for now.)

IT'S NOT PERSONAL

NASA recently announced there are elements in the clouds of Venus that could be tied to life at some point in the future. Everyone is so excited about that, but stop for a minute and look around. You can literally put a seed in the soil here, it eats sunlight for energy, and then water falls from the sky to give it fuel, and it somehow knows how to grow into a strawberry field that gives us the nutrients to sustain life.

WHAT?!? Where's the excitement for an incredible feat like that?

Or what about this: imagine we discovered one of the other two hundred quintillion planets had humans just like us living there. Everything was the same: they looked like us, spoke similar languages, drove cars, and had jobs—but for whatever reason, they had no animals. If they got on a spaceship, came to Earth, and saw a pet dog, they would be blown away. Their jaws would drop, and they'd claim we live with furry aliens. They would be completely overwhelmed and awed by what seems so ordinary to us.

Or just think about what might happen if we could only see the stars one night a year. What kind of curiosity and awe would that spark? What a spectacle that would be—a worldwide celebration! But because we're so used to seeing stars every night, we overlook the constant beauty and the wonder they bring to our world.

The fact is, we live on a planet with stunning mountains, oceans, art, music, food, and connections—not just evidence of a gas that might mean life might be possible on it someday—but we're so accustomed to it all that we stop seeing the magic right in front of us. We should be celebrating the fact that we're alive every day. Except most of us don't.

Instead, we're in pain because the external world isn't showing up how we want it to. We're stuck on an idea of how life *should* be and think the world has to look a certain way for us to be happy. And when it inevitably doesn't bend to match our plans and desires, we're unhappy and can't seem to get over it.

But think of it this way: there are 7.7 billion other people on the planet who also have a personal preference for how the world should be. Every person's preferences are based on experiences and ideas they were taught in childhood, at school, through friends or cultural norms, and whatever and whoever else has shaped their views on life. No two people are even close to being the same, and everyone brings a unique perspective. So, expecting this grand, cosmic piece of art—something so complex it's almost beyond comprehension—to show up in a specific way for every one of us doesn't make much sense, does it?

The universe knows nothing of your preferences or those of the other 7.7 billion people out there. It's just a natural cosmos, doing what it does. There's nothing personal about it. You are a participant in a grand arena that is the result of natural cause and effect.

GO WITH THE FLOW

The ancient Chinese philosopher and founder of Taoism Lao Tzu once noted, "Nature does not hurry, yet everything is accomplished." The earth is four and a half billion years old, and without any human involvement, we have an atmosphere that blocks deadly solar rays. We have rain that grows plants. We have food that sprouts from the dirt. We have animals. We have beaches. The universe clearly knows what it's doing, and to think that our human brains know better how to manage what happens here is simply laughable.

Once we truly understand and accept that the world doesn't have any obligation to unfold the way we want it to, we can start to enjoy the experience in front of us without trying to change it. This isn't an invitation to quit or stop putting effort into our lives. It simply means we should try our absolute best and learn to be okay with how life unfolds without getting attached to attaining any specific result.

Life is just a collection of moments. ^FEET When we cling to a moment—thinking everything needs to stay exactly like *this* for us to be happy—we feel let down when it naturally doesn't linger on forever. And when we resist moments, we push the natural flow of life away and don't give ourselves the opportunity to watch the universe do its thing. Clinging to and resisting moments only inflicts needless pain and ruins what otherwise would have been more beautiful moments to add to our collection.

We just need to surrender to the flow of life. I don't mean surrender as in *giving up*. Life is asking us to engage with it, so we can't just sit around doing nothing. We need to trust that life is always trying to teach us and give us direction, so we can maximize our human experience and put our true *KB* talents on display. Participate in life!

Most suffering happens because we're stuck on an idea of how life is "supposed" to be. *Let it go.* We're not the center of the universe, despite our futile attempts otherwise. Stop resisting what is, go with the flow, and watch life unfold for you.

The truth is, we're only visiting this planet. Life happened before we got here, and it's going to continue on after we're gone. Ninety-three percent of all humans who ever lived are dead. Congrats on being part of the 7 percent of people who are living now, against all odds.

Whenever you're looking for perspective, just zoom out. Consider the 13.8 billion-year path the universe had to take for us to even be here. Think about everything that needed to happen for you to get here—Great-Great-Great Grandpa had to meet Great-Great-Great Grandma, and so on.

Clearly, being human is the ultimate gift, and it's time to start living that way.

CHAPTER TWO

WHAT'S YOUR STORY?

Right now, you might be thinking, *Yeah, yeah. It's crazy that we're alive. I guess I'm just an ungrateful, miserable person for not being happier about it.*

I actually have a better (and kinder!) explanation for it: the reason you're not happy yet is that life isn't going the way you thought it would. You told yourself a story about how things were "supposed" to be. Your family, community, religion, and culture all piled on top of that. And that story just isn't playing out how you thought it would.

Maybe you're consumed with getting what you want, and you're afraid you're not going to get it. Or, the opposite might be true. You're anxious about something you *don't* want, and thinking about how it *might* happen is debilitating. Either way, that's what's keeping you stuck.

So often, our expectation of what we need to become and accomplish before we can feel valuable or "enough" is completely overwhelming. We think we have to achieve something outrageous, like starting a massive business or having the perfect family before life can really begin. We imagine there's some enormous finish line we have to cross, and until then, we'll just have to suffer, grind—or as the saying in the Mormon church goes, "endure to the end"—before we can enjoy our lives.

But as we just found out, the universe isn't here to fulfill 7.7 billion people's expectations. So even if we do all the "right" things—go to a great school; get all the best internships; land a lucrative job; marry a smart, cool, hot partner; and spawn an adorable pack of kids—it's still pretty unlikely our life is going to look and feel how we imagined it would. It's just not very likely because the universe isn't personal.

Besides, there is no finish line. We're valuable even without giant accomplishments. And our worth isn't tied to any specific outcome. Our story about what life is supposed to be is what's actually keeping us from feeling a deep sense of gratitude, connection, awe, and wonder in the world and enjoying our lives now, in the present.

So, mystery one solved: your story is your problem.

ONCE UPON A TIME...

Actually, I should say *stories.*

Because not only do we get tangled up in stories about how the world has to show up for us to be happy, but we also tell stories about ourselves *to* ourselves. These stories go back to when we were kids, can be conscious or unconscious, and are usually fueled by traumatic experiences or the way we saw things unfold. We internalize these experiences, attach a story to them, and continue to believe whatever we decided they meant at the time—even though that story doesn't represent reality now and probably never did.

The underlying theme of all our personal stories is that we're not good enough. Something is wrong with us. We're unworthy of love. None of which is true, of course.

Most people don't even know they have a story, never mind how much it's still impacting their life. But when we carry these traumatic childhood stories into adulthood, they become a filter for all our experiences and start to affect everything we do—and we don't even realize we're doing it! For example, if your dad was an alcoholic who hit your mom any time she called him out on being drunk, you might start to think speaking up is a risky behavior to avoid at all costs.

You subconsciously learned, *If I speak up, I get hit.* And because of the way you were raised, you might stay silent in tough situations even after you grew up and moved out. But since using your voice isn't inherently dangerous—it's actually healthy!—letting that old story run your life is probably what's holding you back from being as happy or fulfilled as you could be.

Social media has only upped the ante for the stories we tell ourselves. Many women feel like, *If I'm not skinny, have big boobs, and travel the world like all those influencers, there's something wrong with me.* Guys lose confidence if they aren't showing up in the world like Gary Vee and try to make up for not running a tech company by the time they're thirty by driving a flashy car or exercising their way into six-pack abs.

To truly level-up in life, we have to work on unpacking and dismantling our stories. We need to see them as the warped view of reality they always were. And we need to start seeing ourselves for who we truly are.

THOSE DAMN SHORTS

For me, it all started with an offhand comment at recess when I was in second grade.

The brand of shorts everyone was wearing that year had the size emblazoned on the front of one leg. Mine were an extra-large. We were at recess doing dog piles when a sixth-grader wearing a size small walked over, pointed at the label, and said, "You're four grades younger than me and wearing a size three times bigger than me. You really are a little fat boy, aren't you?"

From that day on, I took on the "fat kid" label as truth. Subconsciously, I thought, *Something's wrong with my body, and therefore, I'm unlovable.* That story played out for the next two decades without me even being aware of it.

In junior high, I felt like I had to be funny and overly nice to everyone I met. I was totally aware that, as the fat kid, I was at an immediate disadvantage—especially with girls. I wanted them to like me the way they liked my friends (you know, *that* way). No such luck. I thought, *If only I was skinny, girls would be interested in me, my life would be great, and I would finally be happy.* I still have vivid memories of lying in bed with tears in my eyes, thinking that losing weight would solve all my problems. I would have done anything not to be the fat kid anymore.

In my early twenties, my skewed self-image drove me to prove my worth through financial success. I made $1 million by the time I was twenty-four. This led me to create another story: that I was valuable because I was a good salesman. I got so much validation from being successful in business, it became my entire identity.

I believed the only way women would see my value was

through my money, so I took them on extravagant dates. My typical first date move was to pick up a woman in my brand-new one-hundred-thousand-dollar Mercedes and take her to the nicest steakhouse in town, followed by front-row seats to the Utah Jazz. If we got as far as a third date, I'd fly her to Disneyland for the day.

Eventually, I ended up dating Erin, a CrossFit superstar. I spent a ton of money on her, trying to convince her that I was worthy of her love. I thought, *If this hot fitness mega-babe is into me, then the rest of the world will be too.* That's clearly the wrong reason to be in a relationship with someone, and not surprisingly, things didn't turn out well for us (as you'll find out later).

In all my romantic relationships, I was basically screaming, *Validate me! I know something's wrong with me. Tell me I'm lovable because I don't love myself.*

Since I've always had a passion for sports and travel, I also started going to every major sporting event. I always flew first class and sat in the best seats. I'd wake up on a Sunday morning in Salt Lake City, buy a ticket to see the Cowboys or the Broncos play, and fly out and home again on the same day. I was on the sidelines for the Alabama-Auburn game. I hung out courtside with former NBA star David Robinson watching LeBron James play in the NBA Finals. Football, baseball, basketball, any kind of ball—wherever a great game was being played and no matter the cost, I went. Like my own hype master, I posted my every move on social media and basked in the validation that rolled in.

One time, I even spent $15,000 on a ticket to the Superbowl that got me into the same luxury suite as basketball superstar Kevin Durant. Of course, I had to get a picture with him, which I immediately posted on Instagram. But even though we talked the whole game, I was too worried about how much engagement my post was getting to enjoy any of it. It ended up being one of the greatest Superbowls of all time, and I missed it because I was obsessed with watching my likes go up.

Two weeks later, I spent another $5,000 for a ticket to the NBA All-Star Game in New York. Instead of being excited, all I felt was pressure. I had to go, or everyone would wonder why I wasn't there. I remember being on my flight to JFK and realizing the only reason I was on that plane was so I could post a picture on social media. I wished a huge blackout would take down the entire Internet, so I could just skip it, turn around, and go home. Instead, I went, got a pic with Kevin Hart and Nicki Minaj in the background, and continued to watch the likes roll in.

I was starting to wonder what I was doing with my life. Or, more accurately, what I was doing *wrong* with my life since I seemingly had everything and was still miserable—not that

I let a little existential angst slow me down. I kept going like that until I fell into a quarter-life crisis.

Eventually, I could barely get out of bed. I started having panic attacks. I even struggled with having zero motivation to work.

I had everything money could buy, but I was lost, depressed, and didn't know who I was anymore. I was the top salesperson at my company—where everyone referred to me as "The King"—but I hated myself. I was dating a slew of attractive women, but they couldn't fill the deep, dark, seemingly bottomless void inside me.

And it all went back to a story I let get in my head twenty-plus years earlier, on the playground in elementary school. Ridiculous, right? And yet, we all do some version of this.

P.S. LIFE (PRE-STORY)

There was a time when we all lived life without a story.

When we were three, four, and five years old, we'd be on the playground in a complete fantasy world, laughing, jumping, going down the slide, making friends with complete strangers, sharing our peanut butter and jelly sandwiches. We were completely present. We dressed up as superheroes and didn't care what anyone thought.

Think of that version of yourself. How fun were they? *Tons.*

We weren't thinking about what was happening later that day, what was for dinner, or what anyone else thought about us. No one expected us to be a certain way—we didn't even expect *ourselves* to be a certain way. We just *were.* That's when we were our truest, most natural, authentic selves.

So, what happened to all that childlike wonder and excitement?

We went through traumatic experiences. We started to put labels on ourselves. We decided we weren't good enough. We got stuck in a box.

Along my spiritual journey, I discovered the profound healing benefits of psychedelics on the mind (more on that later!). In one sacred plant medicine ceremony, I was shown how we all start life as a massive ball of light and then drop from space into a human body. The message I got was that our whole purpose on Earth is to turn up our lights as high as they will go and share them with other people.

During my trip, I saw the sun shining so brightly. Kids beamed from ear-to-ear, skipped down the street, smelled flowers, ate candy, and played hopscotch. They were fully present, connecting, laughing, and loving. Life was pure joy.

But then, as the kids got older, they started having intense experiences like getting hit by their parents, losing a friend, or being told they weren't good enough, and their lights started dimming. It was almost like there was a knob in the middle of every human that could be turned up or down. After a while—say, by the time they were junior-high or high-school age—the light had gotten so faint, they started to build walls around it to keep it safe and spent the rest of their lives hunched over, arms across their chests, guarding the little light they had left.

What I took away from this experience is that we all love our light and want to protect it. Our light grows weaker when we are in pain, and as a result, we hide it because we're scared of losing it altogether. But that goes against everything we're supposed to be doing while we're here!

There is so much beauty when we share our light. My goal is to help everyone rediscover theirs and show it off. So, how do we crank it back up? How do we get back to our truest, most authentic selves? How do we free ourselves from our stories?

Let's work together to flip the switch and live like we used to when we were kids.

UNPACKING YOUR STORY

Let's start by finding out where our stories started. Like I mentioned before, most stories boil down to, *I'm not good enough. I'm not smart enough. I'm not pretty enough. I'm broken. I'm unlovable.*

But believe me, we're all enough. And our stories are way too much.

Method One: First Conscious Memory

A good way to find your story is to think about your first conscious memory. That's where you'll discover when you first "learned" your story, formed that belief, and created a negative thought pattern.

For instance, maybe you got a C on a math test in third grade, and your friend made fun of you about it. That's the exact moment you learned you weren't smart enough. Now, twenty years later, it's showing up as, *Who am I to start a business? I'm stupid!* And the story plays out, over and over, in all sorts of situations, all because of a bad moment in third grade.

The fact that you still remember the test and the friend teasing you about being dumb means that's where your story started. Otherwise, that memory wouldn't have been imprinted and implanted in your brain. There are so many experiences in your life that are no longer there, but you clung to that one for a reason.

Once we accept a story as true, we subconsciously repeat it in our heads all the time. We look for situations where the story fits and begin wrapping our identity around it. We basically make our story a reality when that never had to happen in the first place.

Let's use my "fat kid" moment to play this out further. One of my first memories is of Playground Phil. My generic black athletic shorts with the white stitching on the left leg were comfortable, and I didn't think twice about them until Phil mentioned the size disparity between mine and his. Once he called me a "fat boy," I accepted the story and never forgot it.

Because I put that story onto myself and took on that label, my relationship with myself changed from that day forward. My self-talk turned into: *What's wrong with me? Why am I the fat kid? Why am I not lovable? If I'm not lovable for who I am, how do I earn that love?* And things just spiraled from there. I let that moment negatively impact my life for the next twenty-two years.

Method Two: Finding Your Shame

Pinpointing where we feel the most shame is also a good way to discover our stories. Ask yourself: *What would I be deeply embarrassed to have someone find out about me? What secret am I hiding that I never want people to know?*

For me, it was being sexually abused by my best friend when I was six years old. It wasn't malicious—he was just curious—but I felt so violated, scared, and embarrassed. In the Mormon church, you get baptized when you're eight, and I remember thinking, *When I'm eight, I'll be forgiven of this sin. I've done such a terrible thing.*

Once I was baptized, I thought, *Okay, at least now I'm not responsible for this anymore,* but it's not like the memory of what happened ever completely went away. There was still so much guilt attached to the experience, I didn't tell a single person. It was the deepest, darkest secret I could ever imagine having. I stuffed it down as far as it would go, locked it up, and tried to never think about it again.

Then, when I was fourteen, that friend got in a car accident and died. It was absolutely tragic, but my first thought when I heard the news was relief rather than sadness (which is incredibly sad in itself). At least now, no one would ever know. Our secret had gone to the grave. I thought I was free.

But even his death couldn't erase my shame. I had a really difficult time making male friends growing up and hung out almost exclusively with girls because I felt like they were safe and easy to be around. Whenever I met a new guy, I would always make a point of talking about all the hot girls I was dating because I didn't want them to come on to me. Subconsciously, I'd created a deep-rooted story that all men were going to hurt me, and I was always trying to protect myself from them.

Ayahuasca finally helped me identify and heal that story. I dropped into the ceremony, and all of a sudden, I was a kid walking up the street to my best friend's house. The next thing I know, I was in his basement reliving those experiences. I remember thinking, *Don't go down this deep, dark hallway*, but I needed to finally deal with the trauma once and for all. It was such a breakthrough, and ever since then, I've met a slew of new guy friends. They've been a truly welcome addition to my life.

As Carl Jung said, "Until you make the subconscious conscious, it will direct your entire life, and you'll call it a fate." I obviously didn't know when I was six years old that locking my shame away would affect me well into adulthood. But because I did, I missed out on having male friends for way too long. Once I was free of that story, it opened me up to a whole new level of life experience.

This isn't a plug for using ayahuasca as a way to heal your stories (if you decide to do it, I definitely recommend using extreme caution—see Chapter Four for more details on that). It's mostly just encouragement to take a look at what you think of as your darkest secrets and see what you find there.

Zooming Out from Your Story

Once we've found the origin of our story, we can zoom out to get a better look at what *really* might have been happening—not what we told ourselves was happening in the moment, but other possible explanations. To do this, ask yourself:

- Where was I?
- How old was I?
- What happened?
- What labels am I putting on myself?
- What did that make me believe about myself?
- What could have been the motives behind the other person's actions?

Using me as an example again: I was at recess in elementary school. I was in second grade, and an older kid called me a "fat boy," which made me label myself as the "fat kid." That made me feel like there was something visibly wrong with me and that I was unlovable.

Zooming out, I can see it's possible that Phil might've felt really inadequate about being such a small kid for his age. It's possible he was projecting his own insecurity onto me. And more likely than not, that situation wasn't even about me in the first place. It wasn't personal.

Here's another example: When a client of mine was in

second grade, she was sent to a third-grade classroom for several subjects because of her advanced reading skills. One day, a girl in that class turned around and hissed, "Everybody here hates you and your stupid boy haircut."

The story my client created from this event was, *Oh no! I'm the annoying smart kid. I guess it's better to hide my talents than make other people dislike me for them. Also, my hair is totally ugly!* She let that story play out for the next thirty years, even as she became a published author. She constantly downplayed her accomplishments and abilities for fear that people would hate her if she showed the least bit of pride in them. Her standard author talk was even titled "Bad Hair, Big Dreams."

I did this exercise with my client to help her reevaluate the situation. She discovered—to her delight—that she wasn't actually ever the "annoying smart kid" after all. Together, we explored other options: Maybe the fact that my client was a year younger made the other girl feel dumb because she had dyslexia and needed *extra* help instead of being advanced for her grade. Or maybe she had a terrible home life, was bullied by her siblings, and they said the same kind of hurtful things to her about her intelligence and hair.

We feel our stories so intensely, we often assume everyone thinks the same way as we do when they don't. People are so caught up in their own shit. They project their own trauma onto every situation to try to make it fit their worldview. They're too busy seeking validation for their own core wounds to worry about us. So, the truth really is, our stories have nothing to do with us and everything to do with them and their lives.

Just remember, things aren't always what they seem—especially so many years after the fact. What you took out of a situation as a child probably isn't accurate, so it's important to look again at what happened with adult eyes. Reevaluate your stories and realize there's more to the picture than you ever knew.

Asking the Right Questions

It's profound how deep of an impact our conscious and subconscious stories have on our lives, even so many years later. Considering alternative interpretations than your initial conclusion can really help put a different spin on things and stop feeding into our stories (because we all have more than one). For every story we uncover, it's useful to ask:

- Where did I learn that?
- Is it true?
- Is there something I'm assuming about the situation?
- Is it possible I'm missing information?
- How might someone else view the situation?
- Is it possible my perspective is wrong?

- What would the opposite perspective look like?
- What would happen if I didn't identify with this story anymore?

Let's go back to me being the "fat kid"—I thought I had to look a certain way and be a certain weight to be lovable—to show how this can help you reinterpret your stories.

Where did I learn that? From the media, social norms, and what I saw play out in junior high.

Was it true that, for me to gain love, I had to be skinny? I mean, no. Obviously, people of all sizes are loved.

Was I assuming something? Yes. I was assuming my value as a human was tied into physical appearance.

Was it possible I was missing information? Yes. Value comes from qualities other than just physical ones.

How might others think of the situation? I'm sure people saw value in me for being smart, creative, funny, loyal, and a good friend.

Is it truth or opinion that my value is based on physical appearance? That's an opinion. It's not true.

What would the opposite perspective look like? I know friends who are really fit, and they also feel like they're not valuable and struggle with self-worth.

What would happen if I didn't identify with this story anymore? I could feel free and have permission to be my truest, most authentic self.

Looking at it from this new kind of perspective, it doesn't make much sense to let our stories get in the way of our happiness. Something that happened to us as a child—and most likely didn't even have anything to do with us in the first place—shouldn't be allowed to continue to run our life. It would definitely serve us better to release the story.

So, be brave. Go straight to the core wound. Once we pin-point what that is, we can finally start to move forward in life. Healing our story is what gives us the confidence to take that next leap.

MAKING MORE STUFF UP

But wait, there's more.

Not only do we conjure up stories about our own lives and our own selves, but we create them for other people too. We imagine what they're thinking and what their intentions are when the truth is, we have absolutely no idea. Then, we play out these imaginary scenarios and torture ourselves for no reason because these stories are fictional. We make them up in our own heads.

For example, let's say it's your anniversary dinner, and your husband was supposed to meet you at the restaurant at 7:00. It's now 7:10, he's not there, and you're all by yourself. He's never late, so your mind starts to race. *Who is he with? He's probably cheating on me! I always knew I'd end up divorced.*

Then, he runs in at 7:15, completely drenched. He explains he's late because he was changing a tire for an old lady who had a flat on the highway. Instantly, all the stories you were telling yourself vanish. Now you're thinking, *He's the best guy in the world; I'm so lucky to have him as my partner!* But for ten minutes, you were in total misery inside your head.

Whenever you find yourself assigning thoughts and intent to someone else, remember: it's just a story that has nothing to do with reality. It probably never happened. And it's not worth the unnecessary pain it causes.

FINDING EMPATHY IN A WORLD FULL OF STORIES

And as if having stories about ourselves *and* other people isn't complicated enough, each of us also has a story of how the *world* is supposed to be. The depth with which we believe in our worldview is one of the biggest factors contributing to the extreme division in the world today. It's what makes people believe, if we're not a particular religion, we're a bad person or that everyone should take a particular stance on hot-button issues like abortion, climate change, or public health.

In 2019, an independent study called *The Perception Gap: How False Impressions are Pulling Americans Apart* showed that approximately 80 percent of the Republicans polled used the words "brainwashed," "hateful," and "racist" to describe Democrats. Similarly, nearly 80 percent of Democrats in the study assigned those very same descriptors to Republicans.

But do someone's political views *actually* make them brainwashed, hateful, and racist? I certainly don't think so. People who believe something different than we do are just basing their worldview on the experiences they've had.

And what would it look like if we actually held the opposite worldview? Would we then be brainwashed, hateful, and racist? Clearly, the answer is no.

Always keep in mind that the same conviction we have around our own worldview is matched with a similarly strong conviction by people holding the opposite point of view. As a (former) Mormon, I was indoctrinated to believe ours was the only true church on Earth. A very common phrase in the religion is, "I know this church is true." But as much as the several million Mormons worldwide "know" that their church is true, I would also imagine every Hindu believes the same about their religion. Ditto for the Catholics, Muslims, Buddhists, and so on. And we all can't be right about that now, can we? Yet, everyone is always so sure *their* way is the *right* way.

If we can come at it from a different angle—that everyone is just deeply rooted in their own worldview story—it allows us to show up in the world with more empathy, calmness, and understanding. We can actually meet people where they are. [We all have so much more in common than not, and someone's particular worldview shouldn't be what's keeping us from making more pure, genuine connections.] *Be kind to people* ✳

This is why I advocate approaching every conversation and every person with empathy. We don't know the personal trials people have gone through to make them believe what they believe. There's a reason they have their story, and everyone's entitled to their own opinion.

RELEASING IT BACK INTO THE UNIVERSE

So, now we know:

It's not the lack of funding in your business that's holding you back.

It's not that you're not sexy enough to have a partner.

It's not that you don't have an idea to write a book.

It's not that everyone else's worldview is wrong.

It's your story! (I mean, *stories*.)

I want you to know that it's okay to have a story. Everyone does. My story was that I was the fat kid. Yours might be *I'm dumb*, or *I'm too quiet*, or *I'm unlovable*. But your stories are holding you back from becoming who you were meant to be.

Being tied to a personal story of how the universe is supposed to be is why we're not embracing the *holy shit, we're alive!* attitude. Our conscious and subconscious stories about ourselves are why we're not in constant awe and wonder at the world. The stories we assign to other people are why we suffer needlessly. Everyone's dogged belief in their own worldview is why there's so much hatred and violence in the world today. And all the above is why we hide and try to protect our light instead of letting it shine brightly like we're supposed to.

Remember, the things that happen in our lives happen *for* us, not *to* us. We all have the power to choose how events and experiences affect us. We can either stay on the path of our stories—the path of shame, guilt, and moral superiority—or we can recalibrate and move in a new direction. It's all up to us.

It's time we let our stories go.

CHAPTER THREE

THE SUCCESS VOID

Diagnosing our stories is a good start, but just because we're aware of them doesn't mean they'll simply go away. (They're more stubborn than that!) Until we defuse and eliminate them, we're in danger of falling into "the success void."

The success void is when people's lives *look* amazing from the outside, but they're still not happy. They feel like something is missing even though they have great jobs, beautiful families, nice cars, and plenty of money and food.

So many of us struggle with this. We're taught that if we go to school, get good grades, and land a good job, everything will be perfect—except that's not how it usually works out. We end up feeling like we did all the right things, and yet, happiness still eludes us.

Because we're tied to a story of how the world should be, we get depressed, suffer, and start looking for an *external* fix for our *internal* problems. We actually try to outsource our happiness to something or someone else: a car, a job, a partner. Twisting ourselves into a pretzel, trying to meet other people's expectations. (Newsflash, none of this works for very long.)

Until we deal with our stories, we spend our lives buying and chasing things that can't give us what we're really seeking—which is to heal our wounds. The real secret to getting out of the success void is by doing our personal work. When we rewrite our stories without all the trauma, we can live a life full of joy, enthusiasm, and excitement. And isn't that what everyone wants?

THE CHURCH VOID

I was born and raised in the LDS (aka, Mormon) faith, and the standards of the church are extremely high. For example, you have to abstain from caffeine, alcohol, and premarital sex, and when you turn eighteen, you go on a two-year service mission. Your reward for following all the rules on Earth is living with your family and God in the highest kingdom for eternity.

My whole life, I'd been prepped for going on my mission—two full years spent proselytizing and doing service wherever in the world the church deemed I was most needed. I thought about it constantly. I was taught it was my ticket to a beautiful wife and family and that no girl would want to marry someone who wasn't a returned missionary.

When I finally got my assignment, I was thrilled. They say the call is inspired by God, and you get sent to where you're "supposed" to go. Well, some of my friends got called to Boise, Idaho, and others to Russia and Samoa, which required learning entirely new languages—none of which sounded appealing to me. But I (and coincidentally, one of my best friends) were sent to Auckland, New Zealand. Even though no one gets to pick their destination, I would have chosen exactly where I was going. It was a dream come true.

Going on a mission is a big commitment and very much a coming-of-age ritual. We followed a rigid schedule while we were there: waking up at 6:30 a.m. every day to study the recommended scriptures and lessons and then venturing out into the community to talk about the Mormon church from 10:00 a.m. until 9:00 p.m. We knocked on doors, chatted people up at the park, went to lunch and dinner appointments, and did service projects.

It was a challenging, full-time job—no watching TV, no listening to music, no playing video games—and it was a job I was excited and honored to do.

I grew up in an upper-middle-class existence, but on my mission, I was living in an extremely basic apartment (okay, honestly, it was pretty much a dump). At home, all my friends were funny and cool, but one of the companions I was paired with was a super-geeky music nerd. It all made me pretty homesick when I first got there, but to this day, I am beyond grateful for the experience because I learned a lot about myself living in a cramped space with someone who was the polar opposite of me, in a lifestyle that was completely foreign to me.

While I was on my mission, I started having a recurring dream. In it, I was looking through a glass sliding door at a white cake sitting on the kitchen counter of an unknown townhouse. I'd get really excited when I saw it, thinking, *Is it someone's birthday? What are we celebrating? What's going on?* Next, I'd zoom in over the white cake and see that it had June 10 written on it in red frosting. And then I'd wake up before I found out what the cake or that date was all about. It was weird but not scary—and also a total mystery. I had no idea what it meant, if anything.

I told my companion at the time about the dream, and it became a big inside joke between us. We'd riff about what was going to happen on June 10: we'd meet somebody who wanted to get baptized in the Mormon church, the world would end, or we'd find the girl of our dreams. But then, June 10 came and went, and nothing crazy happened. (Well, at least on that particular June 10...stay tuned.)

I ended up being close friends with my companion (in part, because we bonded over the June 10 thing), not minding the "dumpy" apartment as much as I thought I would, and absolutely loving the people of New Zealand as well as their country. I felt like I was doing good and worthwhile work and that I was making my parents and my community proud.

And then, suddenly, I got sent home from my mission before completing it.

Nine months in, I started feeling incredibly guilty that I'd lied about living up to all the standards of the church. It was just normal teenage stuff: drinking and girls. But I felt like I hadn't earned the right to be there, so I confessed.

That was the end of my sterling reputation. It was the first time in my life I'd ever screwed up. In high school, I was captain of the football team and student body vice president. I held leadership roles in my church. I was known as a stand-up citizen in my community. Overnight, all that changed.

I was left feeling like I wasn't worthy of being in God's presence. I thought God was mad at me. I believed no girl would ever want to marry me. I was totally depressed. I thought, *I guess I'm not as amazing as everyone thought I was.*

It doesn't happen very often that missionaries get sent home, but when they do, people literally hide in their parent's basement and refuse to go out in public because there's so much shame attached to it. It's devastating because instead of everyone in the church being proud of you, they start gossiping about you. A lot of people even lie and say the reason they came home is a medical or mental health condition to avoid further judgment.

I refused to hide or lie about what happened. I got home on a Friday, and that following Sunday was "Fast Sunday"—basically an open mic for anyone who feels inspired to share at church. I walked straight up to the pulpit and said, "I wanted everyone to hear from me that I'm home. I made a poor decision before I left. I didn't come clean. Now, I'm working on it."

I heard a quote in high school that has always stuck with me: "The best way to stop criticism is to accept it." So, when fifth grade Phil judged me on the playground as the fat kid, I accepted it. And now that the church was considering my actions shameful and me unworthy of completing my mission, I once again agreed with them.

But accepting my criticism didn't mean I'd outrun it. Other people may have eventually stopped judging me so harshly, but that didn't mean I did. The experience created a giant void in me. My new story was: *I'm not good enough.* It was the first time I ever thought, *I really don't belong here anymore. My community doesn't even want me in it.*

THE DAD VOID

My plan was to earn my worthiness back and go finish my mission. All I needed was six months of perfect behavior. I'd go three or four months, get really close, and then screw up again. Girls. Beer. Sex. You know the drill.

I was finally on track to get it right when my world came crashing to an abrupt halt. My mother and father called me into the living room one day and told me my dad had stage four colon cancer. He was given roughly a year to live. The statistical probability of him surviving for any longer than that was basically 0 percent.

My dad was my best friend, and we had a deep and powerful bond. I always felt like I could be myself around him and knew he was proud of me, loved me, and accepted me. I could not fathom what life could ever be like without him and was filled with emotions I didn't know how to begin to make sense of, no less process.

Dad was king of our summer backyard barbecues and always took us on the most fun trips. He was the first one in the stands at all my high school football games and president of the booster club. I never saw my dad argue with my mom—they were crazy in love—and that translated into a loving, beautiful household to be raised in. He was such a safe place and model example of how to support a family and take care of one another.

Dad was also very well-respected in the community, earning the nickname "Coach" around town because he'd coached all my football and basketball teams growing up. He lived with integrity, and in his entire career as a stockbroker, he was proud never to have received a single customer complaint. He always did the right thing and lived a life of integrity. After the bombshell about his health, trying to return to my mission got put on the *way* back burner.

There's a rule that you can only call home on Christmas and Mother's Day during the full two years there—the only other contact with your family happens via email once a week for a single hour. It hit me then that getting sent home was the best thing that could have ever happened to me. If I was still there, I wouldn't really have been able to even *talk* to my dad. Now, I was going to be able to spend the last year of his life with him.

My father did a single round of chemo that kicked his butt. He was well-educated and well-informed and read all the science about his illness. He knew the only thing the chemo could do was possibly extend his life, but that would be at the expense of the quality of it. We were all sitting around at the dinner table one Sunday afternoon when he said, "I'm not doing any more of this. I don't want to be bedridden and sick for whatever time I have left. I'd rather have less time that's more fulfilling than be here longer and be miserable."

You could've heard a pin drop. I felt frozen in time. A rush of emotion started to boil up that I immediately pushed back down. He was basically telling us, *I'm going to let this disease kill me.*

Looking back, I think that's a very honorable stance to take, but at the time, it was so painful and traumatic to hear him say. There was so much uncertainty. We didn't know if he was going to die in three months or a year. I didn't know whether to put my life on hold or start doing something new.

As boys, we're taught to be tough and not show our emotions. We don't learn how to express ourselves. So, when my best friend Scotty called to ask how I was doing, I just said, "Good," like that could even possibly be true. He replied, "I don't even know what to say to you. But if you ever need anything, let me know." I told him I would, but of course, I didn't.

That was the only conversation I ever had about my father's illness with anyone, really. Any time I would start to feel intense emotion rising up in me, I would just completely suppress it. The story I was telling myself at this point was, *I'm a tough football player. I'm a leader at my high school and my community. I have to be strong for my mother.*

Luckily, Dad was pretty much his normal self for the better part of a year. No one would've known he was sick by looking at him or by his activity level. We had lots of backyard barbecues, took trips, hung out, and had a great time together. I will forever cherish these moments and learned we tend to appreciate our time together more when we know death is waiting around the corner.

My dad's disease eventually caught up with him. He started receiving hospice care in our home and soon became unconscious. The night before my dad died, I was sitting on the stairs outside his room with my mom. She put her arm around me, and I started sobbing uncontrollably—for all of about three seconds. And then I just stopped, pushing those horribly painful emotions right back where they came from because I didn't want to deal with them. My feelings felt way too scary and intense, so I pretended they didn't exist.

My father passed away a day later, and I remember feeling shocked that the world just went on as if nothing had happened. It was like, *Wait, everyone needs to pause. We just lost the best man and father there ever was. How can everything keep going like normal?*

After my dad's death, I came to appreciate our tight bond even more. Whenever friends and acquaintances talked about having a terrible relationship with their parents, it only made me realize how incredibly lucky I was to have such an incredible father figure in my life.

Me too!

Still, his absence left such a huge void in my life, it made the one left by feeling unworthy of and unwanted at my church look like a tiny little pinprick. Losing my dad created a new story in me, even though I didn't realize it at the time: *the people closest to me all leave me.*

(people always leave...)

I never wanted to feel that abandoned and vulnerable again.

BRILLIANT IDEA: FILL IT WITH MONEY!

After I got removed from my mission early, I started attending the University of Utah. I was recruited from there to work at the company where I later earned the nickname "The King" and met one of the biggest mentors of my life, Casey Baugh. Not that I was having any deep thoughts about having a soul calling at the time, but somehow, I just *knew* I had to work with him—and I'm glad I listened to my gut. Casey showed up at the exact perfect time in my life, becoming in a sense a father figure to me just when I needed it most.

The first time I met Casey, he handed me a copy of *Goals* by Brian Tracy. I hadn't read any other personal development books before, and it turned a hunger on inside me that I never knew existed. I became obsessed with goal-setting and ended up making $50,000 selling home security systems door-to-door in the six weeks I worked that summer.

All of a sudden, I'd gone from my dad dying—the lowest of

lows—to being basically "rookie of the year" at my company. I had a shiny new life with money and validation rolling in, which—at least in the beginning—felt like it just might be enough to fill the void left by screwing up my mission and losing my dad. In fact, it proved to be such an incredible distraction, I skipped over doing the hard work of mourning my father's death.

Even though I was learning a lot of useful skills and making good money, deep down in my gut, I knew I was only working as hard as I was to attain superstar status in business because I wanted to feel like I was a worthy part of the community again. Financial success seemed as good a way to prove my worth as any. I was always thinking, *I'm the fat kid who doesn't even belong in the church anymore. How can I provide value? Oh, I can make a lot of money. Let me show you have much I have.*

As a top sales rep that year, I earned a cruise to Puerto Rico. I remember talking to Casey on the top of the ship about how I wasn't sure if I was going to continue on in sales because my dad had just died. He told me I had so much potential, I should go all in and commit to working for them for five years. I agreed.

I came home, recruited all my friends, and became one of the youngest leaders in company history. I ate, drank, breathed, and slept work. I went out and crushed it, making over $250,000 the next summer. I was just twenty-two years old.

People were starting to know who I was. I was getting a lot of attention. By the time I graduated from college, I was so all-in on work, I'd literally changed my middle name on Facebook to the name of my company: #DVC.

I made a lot of money and spent a lot of money. I splurged on a top-of-the-line Mercedes, front row tickets to every major sporting event, always flew first class, and took women I barely knew on extravagant dates. A lot of it was just conspicuous consumption. By the time I was twenty-four, I'd made over a million dollars.

By this time, there was literally a cardboard cutout of me at the office, and everyone referred to me as "The King." I was the man, and guess what? Inside, I still felt crappy. Like I wasn't good enough. Like I needed to do more and more and more.

Pretty soon, I was given the opportunity to sell a new product—high-speed internet—for the company. No more selling alarms! I basically raided a Cutco meeting in New Jersey, pitched all their sales reps hard, and walked out with ninety new people who wanted to work for me. Not a single one of them said no to my proposition. I was flying so high.

But just as I was walking out of the meeting, my phone rang.

It was the president of sales. The company had decided they didn't want to get into the internet space after all. Every one of my new sales reps bailed on me except a single friend.

We went to sell alarms—yet again—in California. Inside, I was panicking, and it showed in my presentations. I was just about to close a big deal with a woman in Fontana when her husband came home and kicked me out of the house. Normally, I wouldn't have let it bother me—I'd been through the same scenario a million times. But now I was just so exhausted, I needed a break.

So, I quit.

OR MAYBE FOOTBALL AND A FIANCÉ?

I went home seeking comfort and something else to fill the void. I hadn't dealt with the emotion and trauma of losing my dad yet, so I reached out to a friend who was a high school football coach and asked to join the staff. Being a part of Friday Night Lights was the closest I could get to feeling like he was still alive.

Coaching football was fun, but not nearly enough to fill the void. I needed something or someone else—and that's when I met Erin, my CrossFit mega-babe. I attached all my hopes to her.

Since the only way I knew how to show my value to women

back then was by buying them things, I started spending stupid amounts of money on her. I took her to the Dominican Republic. I bought her a new MacBook. I got her the latest iPhone. I took her on several trips to see her favorite NFL team, the Green Bay Packers.

My coaching salary was no match for my spending, though, and I started racking up debt and missing credit card payments. Even though it gave me hideous anxiety, I thought Erin was my ticket to happiness. I felt like I had to lock her in before she left me, died, or found out the truth about me: that I was a fraud, not good enough, the fat kid who didn't fit into his community anymore. So, I bought her an engagement ring and a Hawaiian vacation during which I'd planned a surprise proposal on the beach. (We never went on that trip.)

My parents had such a beautiful, caring, and supportive marriage, and I wanted what they'd had. To me, getting married seemed (and still seems) like the coolest thing anyone can do. It's fun trips and date nights and late-night heart-to-heart talks with your best friend in the world. The story I was telling myself was that getting married was an incredible adventure. Why *wouldn't* I want to rush into that?

What I didn't realize, though, is that not everyone feels the same sense of urgency about marriage as I do—even if their parents provided a similarly beautiful model of the institution like Erin's had. And as with everything in life, a certain amount of caution is warranted when considering taking such a big step. That hadn't been my biggest strength up until this point and was something I'd have to learn the hard way.

I should have known it wasn't meant to be, but I ignored every red flag and warning bell going off in my head. Even as I put down my credit card to pay for the ring, my soul was screaming, *Do not marry this woman*—and I still bought it! Luckily, it had a thirty-day, risk-free return policy. I brought it back to the store on day twenty-nine. I felt like I could breathe again. I remember walking out of there feeling so light and free.

Until I broke up with Erin, that is. Then, I immediately regretted it all and tried to get her back. But by that point, she'd decided I was right—we shouldn't be together. My heart was shattered.

I bought us tickets to the Super Bowl and pleaded for her to come with me, once again trying to show her the kind of life I could provide for us. I was so desperate, I even started talking to a drug dealer about buying human growth hormone. I thought, *Maybe if my body looks a certain way, she'll fall back in love with me.*

Like HGH could ever fill the void! Everything I did just

made that void wider and deeper and hungrier. I was no closer to happiness by this point than when I was eighteen and got kicked off my mission. In fact, I was about as low as I'd ever been in my life.

THE ONLY WAY OUT IS TO CLIMB OUT YOURSELF

Although I'm grateful for the things I accomplished and learned during my time as The King of door-to-door alarm sales, looking at it now, I can see how the emotion tied to all of this was incredibly heavy and unfulfilling. Back then, I used to think the world had to look a specific way for me to feel happy and that I needed to hustle around to get the entire outside world to match my personal preference. I thought I needed validation from women or to be "the man" at work or to be an incredible member of the community to be considered a worthwhile human being.

I was trying to be everything to everyone: an amazing Mormon missionary leader for my mom. The stand-up student body vice president for my community. The King for my company. The top sales rep, year after year, for my mentor. An amazingly generous provider for all my love interests. How exhausting!

We all have to figure out our purpose on Earth without getting bogged down in outside expectations. We all have to be willing to let go of the person we thought we were supposed to be to become who we really are. Through a lot of trial and error, I finally found out that getting into alignment with who I really was, discovering new skills and talents, and growing personally was the only way to make the hungry void inside me disappear.

So many of us rush around trying to fill the void with relationships, religion, money, and our careers, but we're running a race that's not winnable. When we let other people write our story, we give away our power. And the longer we try to appease everyone but ourselves, the longer we remain unhappy.

Besides, other people's opinions of us are none of our business. Everyone we've ever met has a different perception of us. My mom knows a different version of me than Erin does. Scotty and Nick understand me in a way the girl at the front desk of my apartment complex never will. We basically exist an infinite number of times in people's minds, and it's impossible to satisfy everyone's expectation of who they think we're "supposed" to be. It's time we stop outsourcing our happiness and trying to be someone other than our true selves.

Don't use your energy to worry or stress. Instead, use it to learn, grow, think for yourself, and share your talents. Ask yourself: *How does the world need to unfold for me to feel good? Can I let that go?* Because no one and nothing can make you whole but yourself.

Happiness is an inside job—so I began to look within.

CHAPTER FOUR

FOLLOW THE WHITE RABBIT

So many people have multiple tattoos these days, often turning themselves into complete works of art. I, on the other hand, have a single tattoo of a white rabbit on my shoulder. It's there to remind me that the Universe is always giving me clues. If I follow those clues, I'll find unimaginable truths and rewards. I didn't want that message getting lost in a sea of others (even though I admire those intricate sleeves and giant back pieces you all have!).

It's important to stop for a moment here and note the difference between the scientific universe—lower case "u"—that we talked about in the first chapter and the *spiritual* Universe I'm talking about now. Universe with a capital "U" is what some people call God, the Holy Spirit, Divine, soul, spirit,

Source, intuition, or even just a gut feeling. The word you use doesn't matter, as it all relates to the incredible creator of everything we know and lots more that we don't yet know or understand. Okay, now back to our regularly scheduled programming.

The image of the white rabbit comes from the movie *The Matrix*. The lead character, Neo, is a hacker. It's 2:30 in the morning, he's asleep at his computer, and he wakes up to a strange message on his screen: *Wake up, Neo. Follow the white rabbit.* There's a knock at the door, and the message disappears.

One of Neo's customers has shown up with some friends, and they ask him to come to a party. Neo says no—he has work in the morning. The customer's girlfriend leans in and again urges him to join them. Neo's about to decline when he notices a tattoo of a white rabbit on her left shoulder. He changes his mind.

At the party, Neo meets a woman named Trinity. She eventually introduces him to Morpheus, who presents Neo with a choice. He can take a blue pill, wake up in his bed, and forget everything that's happened that night. Or he can take a red pill and see the truth. He takes the red pill and gains incredible knowledge, and it changes his whole life.

Why am I telling you all this? Because there are things all

around us—right now, this very minute—that life is trying to show us. They might be hard to see because we're stuck in our story, a certain paradigm about how things are supposed to be or rushing around trying to get the world to look a certain way to feel happy. But no one wants to miss the entire show, so it's time to start becoming aware of and following the clues being given to us.

THE SEARCHING BEGINS

I'd already found out that making tons of money and being The King at my company wasn't going to be my golden ticket to happiness—but I still didn't know what was. I wanted in on the "secret" all the leveled-up and inspired people I saw changing the world seemed to know, but by that point, I'd exhausted all my usual resources: beer, sports, women, fancy cars, and exotic trips. I was open to trying new things, so I decided to start following the "white rabbit" to see where it led me.

CLUE #1: BOOKS

You Are a Badass by Jen Sincero was the first self-help book that really spoke to me. She's cool, charismatic, and relatable, and I felt like she was one of those people who were in on the "secret" of a happy, fulfilled life. I decided to start journaling and practicing gratitude because of her. I felt like I had nothing to lose by giving it a shot.

Then, my twin sister Denise gave me Eckhart Tolle's book, *A New Earth*. I was extremely interested in what it had to say because Denise has always been a sort of trailblazer for me: she left the church, established her own business, and started getting into the Universe, energy, manifesting, and psychedelics well before I did. My whole life, it was like she'd been leaving me a spiritual trail of breadcrumbs to follow.

Per usual, she was right on the money with *A New Earth*. Tolle's ideas about being present, living in the moment, and feeling the energy in your body really resonated with me. After reading it, I dug even deeper into the genre by checking out *The Untethered Soul*. I started getting into calming the voice inside my head and learning to free my soul.

My mind was expanding as I kept taking in new information. I wasn't in the place I wanted to be yet, but I could feel myself inching closer. My journey of awakening was just beginning.

CLUE #2: YOGA

Around that same time, I was doing a ton of CrossFit in a misguided attempt to get Erin back. One night after a workout, my CrossFit coach Alli invited me to go to yoga with her. She said it would make me better at CrossFit, so of course, I went.

I felt a little like a fish out of water in that first class because

I'd never done yoga before, but it was a restorative one, so the moves were slow enough for me to do as a novice, and the music was very meditative. Class ended with *savasana*, where you lie on the floor in stillness with your eyes closed.

For the first time in seven years, I realized there was full-on silence inside my head! The whole time I was out there grinding, selling alarms, and building my team, my mind had never shut up or shut off for a second. And now, in the course of a single yoga class, my brain had become totally calm and quiet. I was like, *What is this? How does this happen? I love this!*

Yoga offered me incredible relief from all that noise going on inside my head. I started going to class almost every day. At first, I was nervous about not knowing the moves and people judging me, but the instructors were totally cool, encouraging, and always made me feel welcome. I fell in love with it.

I felt the same kind of soul call to yoga as when I first met Casey Baugh and knew I needed to work with him. So, I bought all the yoga gear—mats, straps, blocks, the works—and went all in.

CLUE #3: TRAVEL

Every November, I make a plan for the upcoming year that

includes an international trip. In the past, I'd chosen to visit Ghana, Nepal, and Peru, and that year I remember looking at the globe in my office, seeing Costa Rica, and deciding that would be my next destination. I didn't know exactly what the country had to offer me, have anyone to go with, or know anyone there, but I wrote it down in my goals anyway.

(Now, stick with me here because these two seemingly unrelated things actually connect in just a sec.)

The University of Utah Utes are my favorite football team, and they were having an incredible season that year. They only needed to beat Oregon to get into the Pac-12 South Championship Game. I—along with all the sports books—was convinced they had not only that joke game with Oregon clinched but that they were going to win the entire conference.

The showdown for the Pac-12 South was scheduled to be played at the University of Colorado the following weekend. On that same weekend, Kanye West was having a concert in Denver, and the Broncos were hosting the Chiefs. What a trifecta! I lived for that kind of action, so I booked a flight and hotel.

Then, against all odds, Oregon totally upset the Utes, so the game against Colorado was now meaningless. Kanye went on a wild Twitter rant that eventually led to the concert being canceled. Except for the NFL game, which I'd already seen tons of, my perfect weekend was shot. I decided to cancel the trip and throw a party at my apartment complex instead.

By the time my buddy Samantha introduced me to the tall, beautiful friend she brought along with her to the bash, I'd definitely had a few drinks. When Sam mentioned Kait was a yoga instructor, I told her finding yoga had changed my life. Kait replied that she hosted yoga retreats all over the world and that her next one was in Costa Rica. (Whoa! Here was some of that synchronicity Jen Sincero talks about in *You Are a Badass*. A clue!)

I bought her 3,500-dollar yoga package and booked my flights right then and there. My reasoning? "I just made it a goal to go to Costa Rica next year, I love yoga, I love Sam, I love you, and I'm drunk." I remember waking up the next morning thinking, *Why did I do that? That was so silly of me. My impulsivity is going to kill me someday.*

When I told the girl I'd just started dating about signing up for the retreat, she said, "No way! *I'm* going to Costa Rica on a yoga retreat in a month!" I messaged Kait, and it turned out we were signed up for the exact same one. Kait told me that, along with the woman I was casually dating, the other participants were two married couples and fourteen single girls.

I thought, *Holy smokes, like, this is going to be like* Bachelor in Paradise! But once I landed in Costa Rica, I had a complete energetic shift. I felt extremely centered and introspective my entire time there. I was so aligned internally that even the girl I was seeing and the other hot yoga babes weren't a distraction.

One night, we were doing a sunset yoga class overlooking the beach, and I found myself in the flow, in the zone, completely tapped in. There was a new moon, and I remember staring up at the stars thinking there must be at least a billion of them. Then all of a sudden, I started feeling super light, like I was floating. I looked down from somewhere up above and saw myself lying on the ground. I started to panic and immediately fell back into my body.

I didn't understand what was going on, so I didn't tell anyone about the experience. I thought I must have been hallucinating because I was in such a deep meditative state or that maybe reading Eckhart Tolle was totally getting to me. But I also thought there must be a reason for all of it: the canceled sports bro trip, meeting Kait at the party I was never supposed to throw, impulsively joining her retreat, and then having such a weird and unnerving out-of-body experience. It must all be leading *somewhere.*

And did it ever.

THE NIGHT THAT CHANGED MY LIFE

I never believed my entire life could change overnight until it did. Literally. One night changed absolutely everything, and nothing has been the same since.

Two months after the yoga retreat, I was on my way home after doing a sales training in Memphis when I got an email saying I had a credit to use on my Audible account. I opened the list of top books, and on a whim, I picked *Stealing Fire* by Jamie Wheal and Steven Kotler (who are actually both acquaintances of mine now). It's about flow state: how to get into it and stay in it all the time. I immediately dove in.

When I got to the part where the authors start discussing the therapeutic benefits of psychedelics like MDMA, LSD, 5-MeO-DMT, and ayahuasca, my jaw dropped. Growing up Mormon, I was taught that every drug basically had meth in it and that if I ever did drugs, I would instantly become addicted, end up on the streets, and then definitely die. But in the book, Steve Jobs proudly proclaims, "Taking LSD was a profound experience, one of the most important things in my life."

I was like, *Wait, what?!?* In my head, drugs equaled scandal, shame, and sickness—and here was this visionary, crediting his business success and creativity to psychedelics. I thought, *There must be something to this.*

A few chapters later, Tim Ferriss, bestselling author, podcaster, and early-stage technology advisor/investor, says, "The billionaires I know, almost without exception, use hallucinogens on a regular basis." I'd always thought Jeff Bezos and Elon Musk had gotten to that crazy successful level because they were in on a secret. It seemed like *Stealing Fire* was letting me in on what that secret was: psychedelics. (Note: I have no idea if Bezos or Musk actually do psychedelics, but it would make a lot of sense.)

A few days after I finished reading the book, my buddies hit me up to go to a cabin party in Eden, Utah, a beautiful little mountain town on a lake. When I got there, I immediately saw Shane, a friend I hadn't connected with since high school, and he offered me some MDMA.

I thought, *I've never been offered a drug other than pot in my entire life, and I just got offered MDMA the same week I read about it.* I would have normally said, "Nope, no way," but I just felt in my core that I had to do it. I had to see what the hype was all about. One of my best friends wanted to try it too, so we took our pills at exactly the same time.

Forty-five minutes later, I was definitely feeling the effects. The music sounded incredible. The lights seemed brighter and more colorful than ever before. I was so into talking to and connecting with everyone there.

I was having a fun time. I certainly didn't think the experience would be life-changing. In fact, I was worried I was headed down a slippery slope. I told myself this was going to be a one-time thing.

Shane ushered me into a dark room where everyone had glow sticks. We started waving them around, watching the trails, and bonding on an entirely different level. Just one time was going to be a tough promise to keep.

When everyone left the room, I stayed behind because I had a feeling there was more to this than just a good time. I knew there was another level—that place where the kind of deep spiritual experiences I had been reading about were waiting for me. I was lying on the hardwood floor with my hands above my head, thinking, *I know there's something else here.*

When I didn't find the key to life or whatever I thought might be revealed to me, I went to stand up again and had a complete *oh shit!* moment. My body was frozen, and it felt like my soul was falling out. It was Costa Rica all over again, except this time I didn't immediately return to my body.

I couldn't say anything—but my brain was screaming, *I NEED HELP; I NEED HELP RIGHT NOW!* Memories from my childhood started flashing in front of my eyes. I knew I was dying, and I couldn't believe my friends were going to have to call my mom and tell her I was dead because

I took drugs. It was a terrifying experience I wouldn't wish on my worst enemy.

But then, just as quickly as it started, I was back in my body and more in control than I'd ever been before. I felt like a superhero. Relieved, I opened the bedroom door to head back out to the party, but instead of landing in the kitchen—I swear on my dad's grave—I found myself in the spirit world.

It was the higher dimension through the veil. I knew I wasn't hallucinating, and I was absolutely blown away. There are no words to adequately describe what it was like because it was so far beyond explanation—but the best I can do is to say it was another dimension layered on top of this dimension. Everything looked like it was in the highest definition you can imagine, and I could see energy floating through the air.

At this point in my life, I hadn't studied any Eastern philosophy or deep spirituality, but the thoughts and visions I was having perfectly aligned with those concepts. I could see the energy inside of everything alive or that had once been alive—down to the wood table that used to be a tree. Every person I looked at, I felt like I'd known forever and could intuit so much about them: their pains, their excitement, their disappointments, their joys. I even saw everyone's auras and light systems in the middle of their bodies.

I thought, "Holy shit, the hippies were right!!"

I gazed out over the lake, and it hit me that I was witnessing the Universe's soul and watching Mother Earth breathe. I saw our planet as being an actual living organism for the first time in my life. *Mother* Earth! I got it now—she's an actual energy.

Suddenly, a beam of light hit the top of the head, blew my crown chakra open (even though I had no idea what a chakra was at the time), and the love of the creator poured into me. It was the most beautiful, euphoric experience. Think of the happiest moment of your life, multiply it by a thousand, and it still wouldn't approach this feeling.

I felt as if I was the most beloved being on the earth, but at the same time, *every* person was the most loved, important creation on the planet. That insane, unimaginable amount of love extended to every living being. The best part about it was I knew I didn't have to *do* anything to earn this incredible love—it wasn't dependent on what I earned or accomplished in life—and it was infinitely mine, all the time, no checklist of achievements necessary. It had always been there and would always be there for me.

Luckily, my best friend Scotty (who was completely sober) caught on that I was having an incredible experience, took out his phone, and recorded me. I kept saying, "I can't believe we did it. We finally got here! Everything is connecting. Everything makes sense now!"

I wondered why no one ever talked about this place. I felt like I could have died at that moment and been in complete bliss for eternity.

I was beginning to realize I was having a different experience than everyone else, so I went to spend some time alone, closed my eyes, and started hallucinating. Now, I'm not claiming what I saw next is truth—I'm totally open to the idea that my brain was firing off random ideas—but this is how I interpreted what happened next.

Before our birth, we all start at a place that basically serves as a General's tent where we run through what our whole life will entail: who we're going to meet, at what time, and what that person is going to mean to us. We make soul contracts with all those people (sometimes, it takes multiple lives to fulfill our contracts), and after everything is precisely orchestrated, we go and play out those experiences on Earth. We have no recollection of this prior preparation during our lives here.

After we die, we go to a giant dome surrounded by more stars than anyone could ever count. The spirit guide there with me—I don't know exactly who it was or if it was an ancestor of mine—told me what I was seeing weren't actually stars, but other planets where different types of human experiences occur. After fully maximizing the human experience on Earth—which can take many multiple lives—we go on with the eternal progression of our soul to this other experience on other planets. In essence, we have infinite opportunities to grow and evolve our consciousness. It was so illuminating, comforting, and beautiful.

YEAH, BUT...NOW WHAT?

The next morning, I called my buddy, who took the same pill at the exact same time I had, and asked him what he'd learned in the spirit world. He was like, "What?"

I rephrased the question. "When you broke through into that other dimension, what did you learn?"

He laughed. "What are you talking about?"

Now I was the one thinking, *Wait, what?* I tried one more time. "When you broke through, what did you see?"

He was like, "Dude, I had a really fun night with my wife. We had an amazing conversation. That's it. What happened to *you*?"

I was forced to admit I'd seen what I interpreted as the entire purpose of life. It was so unsettling to find out our experiences had been so different. I started googling MDMA trips and scoured Reddit, but I didn't find anything remotely close to what happened to me. Some people who tripped on

5-MeO-DMT—aka, "the God molecule"—reported similar things, but I knew that wasn't the drug I took.

The only thing I knew for sure was it was the most real experience I'd ever had in my life. There was no way I could deny what had happened. Without support, though, I was barely hanging on by a thread. I even started sleeping with a nightlight on.

I felt completely ungrounded because reality was not what I'd always thought it was. Honestly, I didn't know *what* was real anymore. I worried I'd screwed up my brain permanently. I remember thinking, *I'm just like all the homeless guys downtown now. They live in an alternate universe, and they don't think they're crazy.*

I was scheduled to go on another yoga retreat around that time, so I invited my new friend Baya to come with me. I'd met her through my sister, and we'd become fast buds since then. I decided to confide in her about everything going on in my life—and brain!—the first night of the retreat.

Halfway through my story, I pulled up a video my sober buddy, Scotty, had taken the night of my MDMA trip. Together, Baya and I watched as I literally glowed while talking about how I'd broken through to the other realm. You've never seen a happier or more amazed person in your life. My exact words were, "There's another dimension of life I never knew existed, and it's *unbelievable!* I've never felt so happy. Everything's connecting. This is *unreal!*"

For the first time since Scotty had sent me the video, I noticed the time stamp on the bottom of the video. Guess what it said—June 10. It was the same date that I'd seen written in red frosting on that cake in my recurring dream on my mission! (To view the actual video, go to www.thedailyshifts. com/june10.)

Baya and I both freaked out, then quickly decided the insane synchronicity had to mean something. I went from being too scared to sleep without a nightlight to realizing life was unfolding for me. Things were happening, and it was imperative that I remain aware and awake, so I didn't miss anything. Since *Stealing Fire* was what had jumpstarted my curiosity with psychedelics, I doubled down on it. I reread the book, signed up for the newsletter, and watched all the YouTube videos.

One day, I got an email announcing a *Stealing Fire* Flow Camp. Guess where it was being held? Eden, Utah—the same place I had my MDMA experience. I remember literally saying out loud, "What the hell is going on?"

I applied for a spot, put another five grand on my credit card, and went further into debt because I just knew I needed to go. At the time, I was still a Mormon sales bro, and I felt like no one I knew in my normal life could relate to what I was going through. The idea of joining a community of people who had gone through similar experiences seemed like it might help me make sense of my newfound knowledge.

I got accepted and drove the forty minutes to camp. But instead of finding my new tribe there, I was an absolute fish out of water. I felt so uncomfortable and like I couldn't relate to anyone. I was the only one from Utah; most of the rest of the group was from outside the country.

This super hippie-type lady with flowing armpit hair asked me what my rising moon sign was and when I told her I didn't know, she looked at me with disgust. "How can you not know your sign?" she asked, shaking her head and walking away. By this point, I was thinking, *What the hell am I doing here? I'm bouncing.*

I decided I'd listen to that night's speakers and then leave first thing the next morning. One of the first people to talk that evening was Kristen, who had just written a book about how not to suppress your emotions. Her teachings were centered on embracing your feelings of fear instead of fighting them. The message really resonated with me.

After the program was over, I found myself walking right next to her. As we headed back up the dirt path to tents nestled among the aspen trees, I heard a voice tell me, "You came here to meet her." I decided I should listen to it.

I thanked Kristen for her talk and asked what she did in addition to writing and speaking. She told me she was a fear specialist who worked one-on-one with clients. It turned out she lived only ten minutes away from me, so I immediately bought a five-pack of coaching from her website. Instantly, that anxious *I don't belong here* energy released.

The next morning, I put all my stuff in my bag, drove home, and booked an appointment with Kristen. The next week, we met, and I told her my whole story. She was in disbelief. She told me she'd never heard of something like that happening on MDMA and that it sounded much more like a 5-MeO-DMT ("God molecule") trip.

Then, she looked at me deeply and said, "Don't be scared. This is actually really exciting because you're waking up. This is only going to happen once in your lifetime."

Kristen instilled a deep sureness within me I hadn't had since my MDMA experience. She brought me back down to Earth and let me know me I was going to be okay. She flipped my fear into excitement.

She told me to pay close attention to how the world was unfolding because I was about to experience a lot of synchronicities. Whether that was through people I met, something I saw on TV, or a spark of a thought, she advised me to follow my curiosity. She said those things would basically be the spiritual Universe telling me it loves me, and I'd be rewarded for listening to my hunches. She turned my awakening into a game, and I can't thank her enough for that.

Before my MDMA experience, my entire worldview was "Salt Lake City, Utah sales bro." After it became, *We live in an infinite universe with endless possibilities.* It was like everything I knew completely flipped upside down.

I even started getting into sci-fi because I was seeing the world from such a different perspective and was excited to see the new *Blade Runner* movie when it came out. The premise is pretty simple: a group of rogue artificial intelligence starts killing humans, so a new batch of AI called Blade Runners is created to terminate the rebel AI. Ryan Gosling plays a Blade Runner who finds a note suggesting there's somehow a child of high interest involved in this battle. He learns that the birth date of this child is carved into a tree in his front yard, so he goes outside and looks at the tree. What does it say?

June f*cking 10!

I remember thinking, *This is a sign from the spiritual Universe. Something big is happening here.* I leaned forward in my chair and started watching the movie even more intently.

Eventually, Ryan Gosling decides that he might actually *be* the baby in question. In his analytical mind, he had always been thinking, *I'm artificial intelligence. The company that created me gave me false memories of a childhood, so I would feel more human and could be more empathetic to humans.* Now, he decides, if he can actually prove his memories really happened to him, he'll know he's that child of interest and not AI at all.

He goes to the "memory maker" at the company producing the Blade Runners and asks how he'd know if his memories and dreams were real or not. The memory maker shows him how she implants memories by creating an artificial scene, telling him he'd know if it was real or not by the way it made him feel. Then, she auto-populates a *white birthday cake with red frosting*—just like the one in my recurring dream! I literally gasped.

I went back to see the movie again the next day and recorded that scene on my phone. I sent it to Kristen and asked her, "What do you think is going on?"

She just said, "I think you're ready for ayahuasca."

A DOSE OF MY OWN MEDICINE

Ayahuasca is a ceremonial tea made from the leaves of *Psychotria viridis* shrub along with the stalks of the *Banisteriopsis caapi* vine. In ancient times, it was used by Amazonian tribes for spiritual and religious purposes. Today, people use it to open their minds and heal past traumas.

The first time I ever heard about ayahuasca, I was driving with my twin sister, Denise, to a family vacation. I'd recently noticed a lot of positive changes in her—while she used to seem pretty anxious, forgetful, and uncentered, now her energy felt a lot calmer and confident. She'd started making healthier decisions like doing yoga. She'd recently left her job to become an entrepreneur, and her business saw great success very quickly. I could see a brightness in her eyes that hadn't been there before. It was as if she was living an entirely new life.

We were winding through the red rocks when she announced out of nowhere, "Hey, I want to tell you something. I recently did an ayahuasca ceremony."

She explained that she'd taken a profound and beautiful journey after drinking psychedelic tea. She said my mom and I were there with her, but we'd appeared as our higher selves. She wrapped the whole story up by saying, "I just have a lot of love for you."

All I could think at the time was, *My sister is crazy, and that's something I would absolutely never do in my entire life.* Looking back now, though, I can see that Denise was once again laying a safe groundwork for me. We have a true "soul contract"—those contracts we make in the General's tent when we are orchestrating our lives before being born—and she's always given me the confidence to stay on my path. I know for a lot of people psychedelic medicine is incredibly scary, but for me, over the course of years, it was as if Denise had been prepping me to be receptive to the idea of experiencing it.

I'm so grateful to her because, by the time Kristen said it was time for me to try ayahuasca, it wasn't a frightening or unknown thing anymore. Still, I was nervous and wanted to know the best way to prepare for it. When Kristen found out I hadn't done mushrooms before, she suggested I start there. A starter psychedelic experience, if you will.

It was going to be my first intentional, true trip, and I had no idea what to expect. So, I got a trip sitter, put a blindfold on, and downed six grams. (BTW, that's not such a smart thing to do. Six grams is a shitload of mushrooms, and looking back now, I see how this was irresponsible behavior.)

Once psilocybin started to kick in, I was greeted by a massive clock the size of three football fields. It was so big, I could walk on the hands of it. Time kept spinning—whoosh, whoosh, whoosh—until it eventually stopped. I think this was to teach me something along the lines of: time is truly an illusion.

On top of the clock, I met a tall, lanky spirit guide. I don't know who he was specifically, but I had the feeling he was safe and I could trust him, so I followed him up an endless glass staircase. I could see a bunch of other people watching me in my peripheral vision. It was like I was competing on a TV game show, and they were there to cheer me on.

Soon, the spirit guide stopped and pointed to his right. A crazy geometric-patterned fractal appeared. He looked at me and asked, "Can you solve this problem?" At that moment, I understood it exactly. I told him my answer, and it was like I'd unlocked the code to keep moving. We continued up the stairs.

Next, he pulled out a difficult brainteaser for me to solve. I had to connect geometric patterns while I explained what I was doing—except not in English. I had to answer in what I can only describe as Universal cosmic knowing. Still, I got it right.

Finally, we got to the top of the stairs and found ourselves in front of a large, grand door. The most difficult puzzle of all was there. I remember trying to figure out what it meant and working on the problem for so long. Eventually, I got the answer, and the spirit guide gestured for me to go inside.

I walked through the door into an infinite library with never-ending staircases and never-ending books. It looked like the *Beauty and the Beast* castle library meets *Harry Potter's* Hogwarts. Inside, there were two high-backed red velvet chairs facing a roaring fire. The spirit guide sat in one, and I sat down next to him.

After a while, he stood up, pulled a book from the shelf, and showed it to me. It was interactive, symbolic, and this particular one starred my mom. I watched as she rode on a school bus with my dad, the bus driver. Together, they were speeding through the cosmos: the road was made of rainbows, the sky filled with stars and my mom having the time of her life. She didn't have too much responsibility— she was just enjoying the ride.

Then, Mom got off the bus, and Dad drove away, symboliz-ing his death. It was devastating to see her waiting there all alone at the bus stop. She had no idea where to go or what to do. She was completely lost without him.

My mom then morphed into a fish and started floundering around. It was the saddest moment I've ever witnessed. Right before it seemed like she was about to die from fall-ing into the depths of the ocean, a bunch of little fish swooped underneath her and carried her back up to where she should be in the water. She was rejuvenated with life again after that. Symbolically, this seemed to be saying that my siblings Ann, Michelle, Jeff, Paul, and Denise and I had helped save Mom from drowning in grief after Dad died.

She felt alone and confused without him, and we helped her rise above it.

The book revealed then that she loves us more than we can ever comprehend; she sees Dad in all of us, which gives her comfort and makes her feel closer to him; she wants to nurture us and watch us learn, grow, and get better; and that once my dad was no longer here, her purpose shifted to spending time doing fun things with her kids and grandkids. This vision gave me a deeper understanding of my mother's perspective. It was such a beautiful moment, I started crying.

Next, the spirit guide pulled out another book. I knew it was my dad's. I was like, *I don't know if I want to go here yet. Do you have another book we can look out for first?* He agreed.

This book starred Lauren, a girl I was friends with but hadn't started dating yet. It showed how we have an incredible soul contract designed to help us both become the best versions of ourselves, how intimately connected we are, and how much she would come to love me. We were symbolized by two birds that kept going in and out of each other's orbits, but as soon as we got really close—basically on top of each other—she flew off and never came back. It then showed how her leaving me would help me grow exponentially.

What's really crazy is this vision turned out to be prepping me for my future romantic relationship with Lauren. We came together so intensely, and then she left completely unexpectedly. At the time, though, I had no idea what any of it meant because none of it had happened yet.

Then, it was time to face the death of my father—something I'd been too scared to look at for years. My anxiety was overwhelming, but I knew it needed to happen. When the spirit guide first opened up the cover of this book, my dad appeared as a lone wolf. He'd grown up in a poor family and ended up being very successful in his business career, and the book revealed how much this upbringing had shaped him. It also conveyed Dad's deep pride in being able to provide for his parents, siblings, and our family, as well as how much he loved my mom and how beautiful their energy coming together had been.

My dad left the Mormon church when I was very young, and the book showed how my dad's purpose switched to us kids after that. He was so proud of us, and he loved us so much. When I was growing up, everyone was always saying, *Oh my gosh, that must have been so hard on your mom when your dad left the church,* but now I got a new perspective. I thought, *Wow, my dad was so brave. He had the courage to step away and live his truth even though that must have been so confusing for him.* In doing so, he gave all of us kids permission to do the same. He was laying the path for us. It was the ultimate sacrifice.

I was then able to see how, when Dad got sick, our family

kept him going. The flood gates opened. All the pain, suffering, grief, and sadness I'd been holding back for so long finally started to pour out. I was sobbing uncontrollably, allowing all the years of suppressed emotion, abandonment, and loss to move through me. It was extremely difficult but also an enormous relief.

Next, the spirit guide showed me how high up my walls were because I didn't want to live through the pain of losing anyone again. It taught me that I needed to be less controlling in life, live in the moment, and stop stressing about how everything was going to end up. I was told I needed to trust the spiritual Universe because there's a plan for all of us in this. And then, it simply said I should enjoy the ride because there are "outcomes [I] can't possibly understand until they arrive."

The very last part of the trip held a sort of warning for me. It revealed that a lot of people abuse psychedelics and don't understand the depths they can take us to. The main takeaway was that psychedelics were put on this earth to heal and better our lives, so we should all treat them with respect.

After it was all over, I remember thinking, *How is it possible that I ate a mushroom and had such an unfathomable experience in my mind?* I got to see these incredible stories and came away with a newfound perspective on my parents as well as an even greater level of love and respect for them. I released all that stored energy and emotion from my losing dad and could finally breathe again. I'd been stuck for so long, and now, I was finally free.

I was feeling the call from ayahuasca now.

MEETING GRANDMOTHER AYAHUASCA

My experiences with ayahuasca are very special and intimate to me. A lot of my insights are private and sacred, but I wanted to share some Universal takeaways in the hope they will spark a lighter, more loving perspective on life in you.

Kristen put me in touch with a professional shaman who had worked with ayahuasca in Peru for twenty-plus years. There are definite horror stories out there, and I knew I was very lucky to have access to the right people, in the right setting, with the right intention. It almost felt like Grandmother Ayahuasca was coming to find me; my entrée to her was so natural and easy.

I signed up to do a ceremony three nights in a row: Friday, Saturday, and Sunday. The week leading up to it, I was instructed to follow a strict, specific diet: no red meat, alcohol, fermented foods, or caffeine. Sexual activities— including masturbating—were prohibited. The goal was to get my soul into pure alignment before the ceremony.

Even as I followed the instructions, I remember thinking, *I can't believe I agreed to do this.* I was so jittery, I had insomnia. The morning of the first ceremony was a gloomy day made even gloomier by my anxiety of having to wait until 5:00 p.m. to get started.

NIGHT ONE

That night, I showed up at the house where the ceremony was being held and was surprised by the different types of people there. Subconsciously, I probably assumed it was going to be a bunch of dreadlocked hippies with a tapestry of geometric tattoos, like the armpit hair lady who couldn't believe I didn't know my rising sign at Flow Camp. But while there were a couple of people like that, it was mostly just "normal" people. A father and son combo. Successful business people. Grandparents. Feeling like I could resonate with some of them helped me let my guard down.

There were very strict rules in place: Don't touch anyone. Don't talk to anyone. Stay on your mat. Dress in all white. The effect was calming and spiritual, and not at all like, *Hey, we're going to go get high and hang out.*

The ceremony began with prayers, but instead of calling upon God, we were calling upon our ancestors and spirits of the world. We asked them to bless us, allow us to have safe journeys, guide our souls, and give us what we needed to purify our lives. The gentleman who was leading the ceremony then burned some sage and began calling us up by name.

One by one, we went up to the altar and kneeled while he poured us our medicine. The serving size was determined by what we'd asked for intuitively as well as what he thought we should take. It was served in what essentially looked like a large shot glass, and the ritual seemed just like receiving a sacrament at church.

I watched everyone drink their tea, knowing my time to do it was coming closer. I remember thinking, *I can still back out of this,* but when the shaman finally called me, I decided to go for it. I held the tea in my shaking hands and took a large dose (I'm a big guy). It was thick like mud and tasted like fermented prune juice—terrible! I chugged it down anyway and knew there was no turning back.

After the last participant drank her medicine, the facilitator poured himself a huge glass and took it. It freaked me out. I was like, *What?! No one's going to be grounded on Earth? There's no safety net here?* I tried to remind myself the shaman had been leading ceremonies for twenty-five years and knew what he was doing, and I was just going to have to trust the process.

We were each given a bucket because the medicine is designed to help eliminate trauma and negative emotions.

We were told it wouldn't be like throwing up due to nausea, but more of an energetic release. We'd know exactly which experience we were purging, and it would be a relief to get it out of our body.

The facilitator started playing guitar and drums and singing ancient tribal songs. Having music as a guide on an energetic level is an incredibly important part of the ceremony because it sets the tone and keeps people grounded. At times, the music is light and upbeat to signify a happy moment; others, it is dark and heavy to denote sadness and loss. The shaman is able to get a sense of where people are on their journey and adapt the music to match their needs. That way, even when participants get lost in the cosmos and the universe is flipping upside down, subconsciously, they can still hear the music and realize where they are and what they're doing.

Nothing happened to me for a full forty-five minutes, but then my trip began. I saw intense geometric patterns that I started dissolving into, which totally blew my mind. This "fractal show" seemed to be the opening credits of what was about to happen, and I was loving it.

Soon, I was introduced to a deep knowing and understanding of my life—it was as if I was watching it from a third perspective. I saw how much I thrive off of pride and love being told that people are proud of me. I could tell this stemmed from childhood and the amazing example my parents had given me—whenever I accomplished something, they always celebrated it.

Ayahuasca then revealed to me that I was now seeking that same kind of validation in business—I was looking for my mentors Casey, Jeff, and Bowdy to say they were proud of me. All my striving at work hadn't ever been about the money or how many accounts I sold. It was because I wanted a fatherly figure to tell me that they were proud of me now that my father wasn't around to do that anymore!

It also became clear I was looking for that same kind of approval in my dating life. My mom has always been my biggest supporter, and that's what I was now looking for in a partner—I wanted to find a woman who was proud of me. This new perspective felt like it would help me pursue my goals in a healthier way going forward.

Next, ayahuasca let me see how being overweight (and the lack of confidence I felt because of it) had hurt me and held me back in life. I never truly felt like I was lovable, so I'd tried to mask my weight by overcompensating in other aspects, like relying on my strong mind and work ethic. Then, it revealed to me that everyone in my life looks at me as being a happy, engaged, and enthusiastic person full of love. They don't see me as the fat kid; they see *me*. I never thought that was the case, and I felt so relieved.

Next, I went inside my body, with ayahuasca giving me a tour of how incredible it is and what a gift it is. I remember pulling off my blindfold, looking at my hand, squeezing it into a fist, and then making all my fingers extend again. I was like, *Holy crap, it's crazy that I can do that. How does it know to do that? I just think, and it does that.*

At that moment, I realized *I* am in complete control of my body. *I* get to choose how I look and feel. If I want to get healthy, I can. If I want to change how my physical body looks, I'm in charge of that. *I* have the power.

Before the ceremony, I'd asked the facilitator for his best advice, and he replied, "Always participate in the experience." If I saw a door, I should open it. If I saw a hole in the ground, I should crawl in it. So, when ayahuasca then handed me a crystal-clear ball of infinite power, I knew I should grab onto it. Holding the ball, it became clear I'd have to bury it to kill the "fat kid" version of myself. Once the ball was buried, that version of me would no longer be necessary. From then on, I'd be in charge of my body and appearance. So, I did, and I was.

The facilitator interrupted our individual reverie to announce that anyone who was not feeling it yet or wanted seconds should come up for more. It was only two hours into the ceremony, and I'd already had two profound, life-changing experiences, so I did what I always do: I made a spontaneous decision. If one shot was good, more must be better, right?

I crawled up to the altar on my hands and knees, downed another large serving, and crawled back to my spot. But as soon as I was back on my mat, Grandmother Ayahuasca boomed, "You shouldn't have done that. You are an impulsive person, and it's going to get you into big trouble. You need to learn your lesson."

OH.

SHIT.

I was in big trouble. She put me into the deepest, darkest space in the middle of the cosmos. There was absolutely no light, no noise, no nothing. I was literally nowhere.

I was stuck in ayahuasca prison.

I knew who I was, I knew what was going on, and I knew I'd taken the medicine, but I couldn't form a future thought or analyze the situation. I'd lost my creativity and ability to think and reason. My core gifts were gone, and I was terrified that my mind would never come back.

I knew I was supposed to participate in the experience but couldn't figure out what that even meant. Besides, there was nothing to interact with, in the least. I remember thinking, *That's it. I learned my lesson—I'm never doing ayahuasca again.*

Just when I was beginning to lose faith I'd ever get out of that hellhole, I remembered a different piece of advice I'd gotten before the ceremony: If I ever got stuck or found myself in a dark spot, I should ask myself, *What is this trying to teach me?* I was told that was usually the key out.

I realized right then the lesson I needed to learn was to slow my roll. My whole life, I've been very impulsive and made major decisions—about investments, travel, relationships—in a split second and never looked back. Although it had served me in a lot of ways, it had also been a crutch. I decided I needed to take much more time to think before I made up my mind in the future.

As soon as I figured out my lesson, I was released from ayahuasca jail and was taken to Sir Isaac Newton's study. I got to peer over his shoulder while he was working on complex equations! Then, I zoomed out and got to see an actual timeline of all math and science discoveries, from the time of Galileo and Newton up to Einstein. At first, the timeline was massive in front of my face, but then all of a sudden, it became the smallest speck and was barely visible to the eye.

This vision showed me how, in the cosmic arena, everything humans have discovered so far is only the smallest portion of what math and science can actually do. The entities guiding me told me in no uncertain terms that we have absolutely no clue how anything works. We literally know nothing.

They used my three-year-old niece, Alice, coming home and putting her art on the fridge as an analogy. Of course, everyone thinks that's so cute, and we all give her a pat on the head for her efforts. That's what they said our deepest, most complex astrophysics equations are like. Then, they said, *Let us show you how cute you are*, and revealed to me a series of mind-bending formulas and equations that are beyond explanation and human understanding. In the moment, though, I completely got it.

(A few months later, I was watching a Neil deGrasse Tyson lecture on YouTube, and he was talking about the probability of other intelligent species in the universe. He said if we found one that is only 1 percent smarter than us, they would think Stephen Hawking's astrophysics equations were cute and put them up on the fridge. My jaw dropped. It was the exact same example the entities had shown me. Synchronicity in its finest form!)

The actual formula that holds the keys to life was then revealed to me. I remember wanting to take it back to the world, share it with everyone, and change humanity for eternity, but an entity told me, "Don't even try; there's 0 percent chance you'll be able to comprehend it after this."

The trip ended by showing me how great my friends are. Scotty and Nick have been my "ride or dies" since I was a little kid. They've always had my back even though we butt heads a lot. Ayahuasca helped me see that if I can remove my ego, I'll discover the deeper truths they're trying to teach me. This gave me even more appreciation and love for them, along with a desire to connect with them more.

The ceremony ended, the facilitator turned on the lights, and we all shared a communal soup. As I was leaving, I said to the host, "That was the craziest thing in the history of humankind. I got some life-changing takeaways tonight, but I think I'm done here."

Ayahuasca had other ideas, though.

NIGHT TWO

The next morning back at my apartment, I woke up and started taking notes about my experience. I was just sitting in my chair, lost in thought, all by myself, when I heard a thundering voice behind me.

"Come back!"

I started pacing back and forth, feeling like I had an angel on one shoulder and a devil on the other, both whispering to me different things about what I should do. My initial decision was, *There's no way I'm going back.* There had been such a relief when I came back to my senses the night before. But then I finally decided I had to, despite my extreme anxiety.

There were a few new people there that night, but overall, it was pretty much the same crew. When I was called up to the altar, I took a single medium dose instead of two large ones. (To this day, I've never gone back twice in an ayahuasca ceremony.)

This time instead of the medicine taking forty-five minutes to kick in, I found myself drowning in the ocean within fifteen minutes. I was like, *No freaking way, not again!* I was being tossed around in the waves, my mind twisting and turning in deep confusion. I was lost. On the verge of a meltdown freak-out. Like there was no way I could survive if I had to put up with this for seven more hours.

It was literal hell.

Grandmother Ayahuasca suddenly appeared before me as an all-knowing entity wearing a big, black cloak. She had a hood covering her face. It became clear if anyone could get me out of this situation, it was her. She pulled me out of the ocean and threw me in a deep, dark cave.

I kneeled before her, beaten, bloody, vulnerable, and weak. I begged for mercy. She asked sternly, "Do you respect me now?" I told her I did and understood she was the beginning and the end.

Her energy totally changed then, and she even got a little

smirk on her face. "Oh, good," she said. "Let's have fun tonight."

She grabbed me and put me on a two-seater rocket ship, and I started speeding through the cosmos into infinity. I saw nebula, shapes, and patterns. It was the most exhilarating fun—truly the adventure of a lifetime.

Soon, I got to a place that seemed to be the capital of the universe—the center of all knowledge and information. I was filled with an overwhelming feeling of familiarity, like I had been there before. It was circus-like in the best way, and there were balloons, purple dinosaurs, jesters, and clowns everywhere. It was truly an odd and weird environment.

A lot of people report having similar experiences when doing psychedelics and call this place "the dome" or "the hub." (My twin sister Denise just calls it "DMT land.") When I was at the hub, I was given the opportunity to jet off into different spokes to learn new things.

The first thing I learned was how egotistical I had been, that I subconsciously had a chip on my shoulder and thought I was better than everyone else. This likely stemmed from what I'd accomplished in my personal and business life, especially making a million bucks by the time I was twenty-four. All of it had given me a certain kind of arrogance.

I was clearly shown that I am not better than any other human on this planet. No one is better than anyone else! I came to know if I lowered my barriers, I would be able to see everyone's humanity as well as learn something from them.

I was told cultivating a genuine interest in others would help me grow, give me a greater appreciation for life and our experiences here, and provide a deeper connection of love. To be the best version of myself, I needed to be open to connecting with all types of people, from all walks of life, with all different experiences. We're all here to help raise the vibration of everyone else. I've kept this in mind ever since.

Back at the hub, I got on another rocket. At the next spoke, I learned how I'd spent my entire life trying to solve the "problem"—from dating to finances and everything in between—and that I needed to stop looking for a solution. In reality, there is no solution. There's so much beauty in the present moment, and that's where we learn the most.

I went back to the hub again and got on another little rocket ship. This one showed me how I am extremely capable of creating beautiful work and, more importantly, that I don't need anyone's approval to go for it. I can absolutely take a chance because we live in a world of endless potential and abundance. I learned I have the ability to provide value to so many people, and I don't need to worry about having a safety net. (At this point, I was dabbling with the idea of

The Daily Shifts, but for whatever reason, I felt like I needed someone's approval for me to make it a reality. This let me know I could just do it now.)

The last rocket showed me how I should seek a deeper connection to Nick and Scotty. It told me to start to ask questions for understanding instead of to accomplish a task. *How's work?* should become, *What's really going on?* I learned that seeking to understand them better would strengthen our bonds immeasurably.

After the ceremony ended, the facilitator commented, "When you walked in yesterday, it felt like there was a cloud over your soul. Now that cloud has been removed."

I left night two seeing the world completely differently. I literally felt reborn. It was the most profound experience of my existence.

I remember saying to myself, *Holy shit, so* this *is what it feels like to be alive!* (Hence the title of this book!) I wrote in my notes the next day, *I feel like I can really see and hear for the first time. I am forever changed. It's beyond human understanding, and I can't believe this medicine exists.*

It was 2:30 a.m. by the time I headed home. I was wide-eyed, reveling in being alive and in disbelief that we even get to be on this planet. I was so full of love and enthusiasm, I drove straight to my mom's house instead of going to my apartment.

When I'd told her I was going to do ayahuasca, she'd given me her blessing, saying, "You're an adult. I trust you, and I trust that you won't do anything to harm yourself." She has embraced all my experiences and supported and loved me through them all. This was no exception. She was captivated by my ayahuasca revelations.

My mom is the most important person in my life. I'm so grateful for her and so lucky to have her. She's very obedient in her Mormon faith, yet I've never felt judged by her or like I've disappointed her, even after I left the church. She is a pure soul who constantly radiates understanding and kindness, and she's made me and all my siblings feel uniquely special. My experience with psychedelics helped me appreciate and love her from an even deeper place and perspective, and I'll be forever grateful for that.

Back at home, I sat down in my inspiration chair to take notes on the night before. I turned on Mumford & Sons, and the music was so beautiful, I started crying. I felt so present; there was nothing else on my mind other than just listening. Every other time I listened to music, there was always an alternate conversation happening in my head. But in this moment, it was gone and what was left was just me and the tunes. It felt like euphoria.

Since then, I've been able to see and hear what's always been there—but was obscured by all my "stuff"—much more clearly. There's a whole beautiful world waiting for us if we can just quiet our minds and open up our eyes and ears.

NIGHT THREE

I was feeling very confident going back on the third night of the ceremony. I decided to take only a small dose of medicine and quickly found myself back at the hub. I kept waiting to get picked up, but no rocket ever came. I was starting to get weirded out because it's such a funky, non-human place.

Finally, I got thrown into a classroom with a chalkboard. An entity started writing me a list.

1. Get out of debt
2. Never gamble again
3. Stop eating meat
4. The Daily Shifts = full mentorship program

There was a practical efficiency surrounding my experience that night. It was as if ayahuasca was telling me: *You've had your life-changing experiences, healed your traumas, and eliminated your heavy energy. We've shown you what life looks like if you go after it without seeking permission and what it feels like to truly be alive. Now, by the way, don't forget these last few things and then go be on your merry way.* The whole trip only lasted two and a half hours, and then I was sober again.

I ended up following all the advice I received that night. I started paying off my bills. I quit betting on sports games, which was a good thing because I had been getting pretty addicted to that excitement. I became a vegetarian and lost forty pounds as a result. And while I'd always envisioned The Daily Shifts as only an app, my thinking about it "shifted" after that night, and it came to encompass so much more: a coaching platform, mastermind group, online classes, one-on-one mentorships—even this book.

A WORD OF CAUTION

A lot of amazing things are happening in the psychedelic space these days, and the science behind the positive influence they can have on our health and well-being is staggering. Prestigious universities, such as Johns Hopkins Medical School and the University of California-Berkeley, have both recently opened research centers dedicated to the study of psychedelics. The results of their studies are nothing short of miraculous for people suffering from the long-term effects of PTSD, anxiety, depression, and addiction. Psyche-delics have been shown to greatly reduce and sometimes even eliminate these difficult issues that pharmaceuticals have never been able to adequately address.

Even for people who are not facing a serious mental health struggle, psychedelics can provide incredibly powerful and illuminating discoveries. They assist in healing trauma, guide us to make better life choices, and show us how to see more beauty in the world around us. Still, people need to be incredibly careful about how, when, and why they are taking psychedelics. Things can and definitely do go wrong otherwise.

First things first: I am not an expert. You should always seek advice from a medical professional before taking any mind-altering substance. Enter at your own risk!

Secondly, I definitely do *not* recommend taking six grams of mushrooms as anyone's first psychedelic experience. Even though I had an incredible experience meeting with spirit guides, encountering deeper expressions of my parents, and seeing things in a new and beautiful way, that's definitely not the norm. I was seriously naive about the need for caution when using psychedelics, so please do not emulate my behavior here. After doing more careful research, I realized I took on a lot more risk than I was aware of at the time.

The purpose of using psychedelics and visiting such a spiritual, healing space is to improve the quality of our human lives, not just hang out, get buzzed, and be treated to trails and trippy visions. A common mistake people fall into when they start experimenting with psychedelics is getting caught up in the next ceremony, breakthrough, insight, download, or visual without ever doing any self-healing in between trips. By my seventh time doing ayahuasca, that was pretty much where I found myself—focused on the next ceremony rather than doing the work.

I felt like Grandmother Ayahuasca kept calling me back, and I kept on going. But even though I always left with great takeaways, nothing nearly as profound as what happened during my first experience ever happened. Realizing my mistake, I went into my eighth ceremony with the intention of saying goodbye to ayahuasca for a while.

I had a lot of anxiety going into it, but it turned out to be a smooth ride. It almost seemed to be an accountability of all the important people in my life: my father, my siblings, all my friends. It was uplifting and heartwarming.

Toward the end of the night, I found myself alone with Grandmother Ayahuasca. I told her, "I really want to live a great life, but I feel like I rely on you too much and have to come here too often." She leaned over, put her hand on my heart, and said, "I am always with you."

She was basically telling me, *You don't have to come here to see me. Just call me, and I'll be there with you.* It was such a beautiful bow to tie up all my experiences. It made me realize I already had so many tools, so many downloads, and so many insights I could use in my life. Getting stuck in going to the next retreat and having the next trip would be missing the point. I decided then I was just going to go be Doug to the fullest after that.

The thing about psychedelics is, they do not solve your problems. They won't fix anything *for* you. All psychedelics do is give you the instruction manual. You're still required to do the hard work yourself.

Imagine you show up to your house, and in your backyard, you find a bunch of wood, tools, hammers, nails, and some pieces of metal. You know you're supposed to build something with all of it, but you have no idea what. You give it your best shot but still can't quite piece it together. Psychedelics would simply help you realize, *Oh, it's actually not a deck; it's a treehouse I'm supposed to build,* but you'd still be the one who had to actually build it.

Another issue that comes along with psychedelic use is the tendency to want to share—and maybe *over*share—your experiences with other people. (Or at least that's what happened in my case.) I became a total enthusiast, reading everything I could about psychedelics, sharing my stories, and encouraging everyone I knew to do it. Looking back, I can see how my expressing my views on these ceremonies came across as preachy. One of the biggest lessons I've learned from this is: my experience is not yours.

In 2019, I got invited to a New Year's party and found myself sitting next to Tim Ferriss—yes, the same thought leader quoted in *Stealing Fire*. Knowing he was also a psychedelic enthusiast made me want to share my stories with him. I felt like no one else in my life got it, but Tim would.

My expectation was we'd be on the same page, share stories, and be high-fiving BFFs by the end of the night. Instead, he didn't match my enthusiasm at all. It almost seemed like there was a look of warning on his face. I felt very shut down, and it didn't make any sense to me. I wondered what I was missing.

The next day, the same group gathered for brunch. Tim approached me and said, "I'm really glad you're taking a close look at these compounds, but they're incredibly powerful. I suggest being careful. I've had friends who got too into psychedelics. They broke and never came back from it."

I have to admit to feeling a little cocky in reaction to his proclamation, like that could never happen to me. I was like, *I've had the hard experience. I went to ayahuasca prison. I was calm. I can handle it.*

Six weeks later, I decided to do a deep mushroom trip by myself. I was like, *I know what I'm doing*, and took four grams. I had an ego that I was a "strong tripper."

I was lying in bed when I started feeling this deep intensity.

It was super uncomfortable, so I kept changing positions and the music I was listening to to try to get relief. I was really hot; then, I was freezing.

Next, I forgot how to do simple things. I forgot who and where I was. I had no idea what was going on. I started to spin out. I panicked. I was frightened, stuck in a place I'd never been before.

And then, I had a full-on psychotic breakdown, falling into an abyss of sheer terror. I knew I was in serious danger and started sobbing. Somewhere deep inside me, I heard Tim's words echoing around my mind: *they broke and never came back.*

I completely lost my shit. It was the most terrifying moment of my life. And if I hadn't taken care of set and setting, it could have been much worse.

In a singular coherent moment, I called my neighbor, Anna, a dear soul friend. She came over and literally saved my life that night. If she hadn't shown up, the result could have been very different. I could have been ruined forever, just like Tim had warned me.

I totally got what he'd been trying to tell me after that. Since then, I've never looked at psychedelics the same. I have a whole other level of deep reverence and respect for them.

The only other trip I've regretted was my second time doing 5-MeO-DMT (the "God molecule"). It's a psychedelic derived from toad venom, and proponents say it helps alleviate anxiety, PTSD, and treatment-resistant depression in a single puff.

The first time I did it, it was amazing, so I figured I was in for more amazement the second time around. Wrong. After inhaling it, I got blasted out so far away, I felt like I was literally in a different dimension. The normal laws of physics and basic understanding weren't applicable, and it was very weird and startling. I leaned over to the shaman, Mary, and said, "Hey, I'm really scared right now. I don't know what is going on."

The thing with 5-MeO-DMT is that it provides only a very short trip, lasting twenty to forty minutes. That compressed timeframe doesn't give you an opportunity to process what just happened in your deep subconscious. As a result, you're sometimes left with a bunch of jigsaw puzzle pieces instead of the full picture of what you were supposed to learn.

For the next month after that trip, I felt super unsettled and unstable. At times, I even thought I was losing a grip on reality. I worried I didn't know what was real and what wasn't anymore. It set off inside me a deep existential crisis. I kept asking myself, *Who am I, and what is going on?* I was so grateful when I finally felt like my mind was okay again.

5-MeO-DMT is a truly different beast when it comes to psychedelics. I really think most people should stay away from it. In my opinion, it should be reserved for people who are suffering from severe depression or anxiety, are suicidal, and have run out of all other options (but once again, I am in no way an expert or professional in this field).

The bottom line is: *these substances are not toys.* There is a potential of things going terribly wrong, without any hope of recovery. Especially if you have a history of mental illness, such as bipolar disorder or schizophrenia, psychedelics are a no-go because they can spark never-ending episodes of mania or psychosis.

Today, I rarely trip—and when I do, it is always in the right set and setting, with the right safety precautions in place and with trained professionals, who know what they're doing, presiding over the ceremony.

I've always believed that if you are called to work with psychedelic medicine, "the plants" will always beckon to you. Looking back, I believe ayahuasca came to get me. Everything from the "breadcrumbs" my twin sister, Denise, left for me to having access to trained professionals in a safe space to my supportive network is a rarity, and for that, I'm extremely grateful.

FINDING A NEW PERSPECTIVE

After my various psychedelic experiences, everything changed for me. Nothing in my life was physically different, but I started seeing things from a completely new perspective. Even the trees in my backyard looked more vibrant and alive than they ever had before. They'd always been there; I'd just never noticed them in that way before. As author Anais Nin once put it, "We don't see things as they are; we see them as we are."

The aftereffects of my experiments in psychedelia are going to stay with me for my entire life. I'm not trying to suggest these substances are the only way to open our minds (again, explore at your own risk!), but I do want to encourage everyone to shift the way they see themselves and the world. There are a lot of different perspectives out there to explore outside that same old lens we're used to looking through.

Certainly, there are many ways to look at the world with new eyes without using mind-altering substances (through meditation, yoga, being out in nature, journaling, breathwork, or anything else that does it for you). All you need to do is find what that is and use it to your advantage.

As poet W.B. Yeats once said, "The world is full of magic things, patiently waiting for our senses to grow sharper." Take the time to slow down and start looking for those magical things. They're there, just waiting for you to see.

CHAPTER FIVE

USE THE FORCE

I'm a big *Star Wars* fan. It's great entertainment, but more than that, the series contains a lot of spiritual themes. (Seriously!)

In *The Force Awakens,* the main character Rey finds herself on another planet armed with valuable information that can help the Resistance. At a crucial point, she's given the opportunity to continue on her journey or go back home. She chooses home. Her parents left to fight when she was a little girl, and she's been waiting for them to come back ever since.

Before she can leave, cantina owner Maz—a wise old woman—tells Rey what should have been obvious to her all along: her parents are never coming back, and they cannot save her. Maz then goes on to say, "The belonging you seek is not behind you; it is ahead. I am no Jedi, but I know the Force. It moves through and surrounds every living thing. Close your eyes. Feel it. The light—it's always been there. It will guide you."

For me, the deeper meaning here is if we can just slow down, listen to our intuition, and trust that it will guide us, it will always lead us to a better future. And instead of waiting for someone to save us, we can use our inner knowing to save ourselves.

The Force is always with us.

THE FORCE = SOURCE

In *Star Wars*, The Force is what binds the galaxy together. It is the mysterious energy field that is part of every living thing. It is a light that has always existed, acting as a guide to those who tap into it.

In essence, The Force is what I refer to as Source.

Some people define Source as God or the Holy Ghost. Others use words like the divine or the Universe. We can also call it intuition, a gut feeling, the soul, or spirit. The word we use doesn't matter. What does matter is believing in something beyond us—something with our best interests at heart that loves us—is shepherding us through the human experience.

HAVING A RELIGIOUS CRISIS DOESN'T MEAN YOU'RE NOT SPIRITUAL

I always thought I had a strong connection to God when I was still in the Mormon church—and then I went through a religious crisis. I realized I wasn't getting what I needed out of church anymore, and maybe I never had. (Don't get me wrong—I don't think the Mormon Church is bad or negative in any way. It just didn't align with me.)

The thought of leaving the church was *scary*. It was where I learned why we're here. Where we come from. Where we go when we die. All the hard questions were answered for me. It was who I was.

Without that foundation, everything I thought I knew to be true was gone. I was left with a lot of questions. I felt like my whole identity was up for interpretation, and I was going to have to rebuild my belief systems on my own.

It was only after I left the Mormon church that I was able to create a real relationship with what I now call the Universe (aka, God/the spiritual Universe). MDMA allowed me to feel—firsthand—the limitless love of the creator. This infinitely superior and wise entity loves us all with the same sense of conviction, and it is a truly euphoric, beautiful, indescribable experience once we realize the depth of this emotion.

Through my experiments in psychedelics, I learned that we

all have access to intuition and the divine whenever we want. Source is always available to *everyone*. We don't have to be worthy. No one has to put their hands on our heads to give us divine inspiration—it's already within us. It's inside *you*.

Every religion, at its core, comes down to the same beliefs: love one another, create a relationship with God, and be your best self. I truly believe that when we die, the question of what religion we were on Earth is not even a factor or topic of conversation. The Universe is bigger and greater and grander than we can ever comprehend or imagine. How we progress our soul, treat others, and spread love are what matter in this life, and a spiritual practice can help us focus on those things.

So, if you're going through a faith transition like I did, I just want you to know that you can have a connection to God without being part of a specific religion. You don't have to go to church, temple, or mosque to have a relationship with Source or feel the divine love of the Holy Ghost. It's not an either/or thing—either I'm religious, or I'm an atheist. You can be spiritual without the formalities and structure of religion, and leaving your religion is not the same thing as quitting on God.

And if you are already part of a religion that is fulfilling and makes you feel connected to a higher power—great! That's what everyone is looking for, and I'm not trying to suggest you do anything differently. In my case, it took going outside of religion to find that beautiful connection, but whatever works is what's best for you.

MAKING THE CONNECTION

While everyone has unlimited access to inspiration, we still have to create a relationship with Source. For me, that looks like meditation. For you, it might be singing, dancing, writing, doing yoga, or going to church. All that matters is making that connection a priority.

Connecting to Source doesn't require any special education or equipment. We don't have to do yoga, meditate for hours on end, or live in a monastery to strengthen that relationship. We don't have to go to church for two hours every Sunday and read the bible every night to communicate with Source. All we need to do is start to notice the way it is always trying to guide us.

Tuning into Source is like tuning a radio and turning the dial to find the right frequency and eliminate the static. Our version of static is what I call noise—scrolling Instagram, watching college football or *The Bachelor*, or playing video games—and it's not that noise is bad. We just need to be aware of it and make sure we're tuning it out sometimes.

Eliminating noise helps us recognize intuitive hits from

Source. When we get really quiet, we start to become aware of the subtle ways it is speaking to us. Tapping into that voice is where we can find divine inspiration.

WHEN SOURCE TALKS, I LISTEN

I changed the course of my life because I listened to Source and acted on the information it gave me.

When I was first building The Daily Shifts app, there was a point where I ran out of money. I needed $40,000 to finish the project, and I only had $6,000 to my name.

For whatever reason, though, I never felt stressed. I felt sure I was in alignment with what the Universe wanted me to do. I just needed to follow the next breadcrumb and trust that the Universe had a plan for me.

One day, I was at my altar meditating and felt an intuitive hit that said, *You need to go down to your old company right now.* By that point, I was trying very hard to disassociate myself from them and hadn't been there in more than a month. I remember thinking, *I'll go when I'm done meditating,* and it was like, *No, you need to go RIGHT NOW.*

So, even though I was only five minutes into my meditation, I took off my blindfold (yes, I meditate with a blindfold on), got into my car, and drove straight there. I had no idea who would be around or what was going to happen. I figured, worst-case scenario, I'd run into an old friend and grab lunch.

Instead, I found my three biggest mentors in a room all together, by themselves. They waved me in and started asking me about the company I was building. I had a beta version of my app, so I showed it to them. They started playing with it and giving me positive feedback.

Then, Casey Baugh asked me, "How much would you sell your whole company for right now?" I told him $2 million. All three of them decided to buy into my company at a certain percentage right then and there.

By listening to Source, I didn't just get the money I needed to finish my app that day; I got a six-figure investment. I used the extra cash to build out my business in ways I hadn't even yet thought of: I added a website, blog, online course, and work-book. I brought on someone to write my newsletter and hired teachers to gain specific knowledge that I share with you here.

And it all happened because I followed my intuition and soul's urge. Surrendering to the Universe's plans for us always turns out better than what we could have imagined on our own.

I think it's important to note here that I had gone into major credit card debt creating the beta version of my app, even though I had no idea how or when (or if!) I'd be able to pay it off. I only knew that the Universe responds to effort and had faith things would work out. If I had only been able to *describe* my business idea to my former colleagues, I would have never received their investment. My commitment to forging ahead and following my soul's urge was what sealed the deal.

TRUSTING YOUR INTUITION

We've all had moments where listening to our gut or intuition turned out to be the right thing to do. These kinds of hunches aren't measurable by science, but they exist. That's Source.

Learning to trust our intuition and acting on what we hear might feel silly or even scary at first. Hunches, whispers, nudges—how can any of those be taken seriously? All I can say is that the Universe is always talking to us and giving us clues. I got a crystal-clear message about going over to my former workplace, and it turned out to be a defining moment in my life.

The Universe will nudge us in the right direction. If we don't act on the hints it gives us, it will eventually give it to us as a brick in the face. Then it's a crisis.

My CrossFit ex-girlfriend Erin was a definite brick-in-the-face moment. I knew the whole time we were together that

I shouldn't be dating her, but I still got so involved I ended up buying her a ring. If I had only trusted my intuition, we both could have avoided a lot of drama and heartbreak.

Another instance in which not listening to my intuition cost me big-time was when I invested in a fund that looked like a home run on paper but was a definite no-go in my gut. I ignored those feelings, even after the money wire wouldn't go through on the first try. I should have realized that the Universe was screaming, *Don't do it!* at me, but in my brain, it made sense, so I kept going. I ended up losing more than 70 percent of my investment.

The Universe has proven to me that I can absolutely trust it, so these days I always jump when I hear the nudge—even if it doesn't make any logical sense. I just know it's the right thing to do.

When we learn to listen to and trust our intuition, it can solve a lot of problems in our lives. We get stronger in our convictions and have more confidence in our choices. Once that happens, we find ourselves in situations that align with the optimal path for us.

Take my friend Charles, for example. He was a homeless heroin addict when he was in his early twenties. He had no money, was squatting in an abandoned building, and had hit rock bottom.

One day, he was wandering around in the forest. He didn't know what it was that was giving him this message, but somehow, he just knew it was time to get his act together. He started by getting a job, moving to another house, and then finally getting the help he needed at a rehab center.

By following his intuition, he kicked his heroin addiction and is now working side by side with one of the richest businesspeople in Utah. He has a beautiful wife and two lovely kids. He's made such a success of his life. And it all happened just because he listened to the knowing within him.

As Steve Jobs said, "Don't let the noise of others' opinions drown out your own inner voice. And most important, have the courage to follow your heart and intuition. They somehow already know what you truly want to become. Everything else is secondary."

MAKING SPACE FOR SOURCE

Learning to listen to and trust Source takes conscious effort and a daily practice. It requires taking action and having the courage to trust the messages you receive.

So, how can we invite Source into our everyday lives? For me, meditation works best. For other people, it might be yoga, crystals, journaling, taking a walk in nature, going for a run, or acupuncture. I have a friend who drives into the mountains, sticks her feet in the dirt, and covers herself with leaves whenever she wants to connect with Source. Pick whatever quiets your mind, eliminates everyday noise, and gives Source a chance to step in.

No one knows what's right for you but you. Sometimes, thoughts, fears, and other people's opinions get so loud we can't hear ourselves. Do what you need to do to get back in touch with yourself and Source. As Rumi once said, "Quiet the mind, and the soul will speak."

Listen for that little voice inside your head. This is Source collaborating with the truest part of your soul. It is the key to your happiness.

MEDITATION TIPS FOR NEWBIES

Anyone—everyone—can meditate. It's not about crossing your legs a certain way, om-ing while putting your fingers into little circles, and trying to meet God. (If you do that, you're going to be disappointed!) It's about quieting the mind and allowing your thoughts to land on new insights and ideas.

Meditation is to the mind what working out is to the body. If someone is overweight and has bad eating habits, one kick-ass CrossFit session isn't going to put them into tip-top shape. But consistently doing CrossFit in addition to adopting healthy eating habits is going to dramatically improve their quality of life over time. The same is true for meditation—you have to consistently practice it to get the benefits.

To get started:

1. Find a quiet spot. It could be an altar with Buddha statues and a meditation cushion, or it could just be a favorite chair. Close the door, turn off your phone, and take fifteen minutes of uninterrupted silence.
2. Sit up with a straight spine. This says to your physical body, "Hey, I'm showing up and being intentional here!" I don't recommend lying down—it's too easy to fall asleep or lose your concentration.
3. Close your eyes. Allow your mind to do what it needs to do.
4. Focus on your breath.
5. Be nonjudgmental. There's no right or wrong way to meditate. It might be uncomfortable sometimes, and that's normal. I've had sessions where fifteen minutes felt excruciatingly long, and I've had others where I closed my eyes and an hour felt like nothing. Every day is different. Bottom line: don't judge your practice. Remember, it's called a practice for a reason.

Things to consider when you're meditating:

• Your life, blessings, capabilities, body, and ability to see, think, speak, connect, move, breathe, laugh, cry, and grow.

- The world around you and the creator of it.
- The oceans, forests, mountains, beaches, deserts, and every living creature on this beautiful planet.
- Gratitude for the force that created and sustains it all.
- A mantra: repeat, "I am loved; I am worthy."

Billionaire hedge fund manager and philanthropist Ray Dalio once said, "Meditation, more than anything in my life, was the biggest ingredient of whatever success I've had." Let it be a part of your success too. Get quiet, listen for Source, and pay attention to your soul's urges.

Even if you don't have time to do a traditional meditation—say you're in your car or at work and you're feeling stressed and anxious—you can still use mindfulness to ground your thoughts. One way I like to do that is simply by closing my eyes, relaxing, and sending out love, happiness, and success to someone I love. Even just twenty seconds of focusing on the joy of others are enough to recenter and recharge my mind. Close your eyes right now and wish for someone you love to be happy. Notice that change? That's what I'm talking about!

If you're having trouble getting started, you can always download The Daily Shifts and try a guided meditation from the app.

WE CAN'T FIGURE IT OUT—AND THAT'S OKAY

If you're feeling like you don't really understand what Source is or how it can actually exist, take heart. No one knows. We can't figure out Source, just like we can't figure out the mysteries of the universe. And that's okay.

In the electromagnetic spectrum, visible light is only a fraction of 1 percent of the entire thing. That means we don't see more than 99 percent of what is actually happening because we don't have the right receptors to perceive whatever else is going on. The same is probably true of our intuition. Whenever we have intuitive hits, there's probably a lot of information that's not getting through because of our limited perception. So, we just have to go with the flow and trust the information in whatever way we understand it.

My favorite analogy: We all love our pets, right? They clearly have emotions, a personality, and a soul. We have a connection to them and love them very much. Yet, no matter how hard we try—even if we dedicated the rest of our lives to it—our dogs will never understand global economics. Given the capacity of a dog's brain, that's just completely incomprehensible to them.

The gap between a dog's brain and ours is probably similar to the knowledge gap between us and the creator. No matter how hard Source may be trying, its knowledge and capacity are beyond anything we can comprehend in the slightest.

If our dogs were trying to understand global economics, we would pat them on the head and say, "Just go fetch the ball." I think Source might be trying to give us the same kind of message. Like, "You can't figure it out, so just go be human. The purpose of life is life. The only way you can screw it up is by trying to solve it."

WHEN YOU DON'T KNOW WHAT TO DO, DO NOTHING

Oprah said, "When you don't know what to do, do nothing." It's one of my favorite quotes.

Back when I was running out of money to finish The Daily Shifts app, I didn't know what I was going to do about it for at least two months. The only thing I knew was that, if I waited patiently while doing the work that needed to be done without getting desperate, I'd get the signs I needed from the Universe. And we all know how that story ended: with a multiple six-figure investment that helped me expand my business in new and exciting directions.

As humans, we're so restless all the time. We want to fix everything immediately. We like action and instant gratification. As soon as we get one thing, we're on to the next.

Sitting still in moments that feel chaotic or scary isn't easy. But when we take time out to "do nothing," things start unfolding a certain way. It gives the Universe time to let things play out and then put them in our path.

As Steve Jobs said (again, I know!), "You can't connect the dots looking forward; you can only connect them looking backward. So, you have to trust that the dots will somehow connect in your future."

Intuition is the GPS of the soul. Remove the angst and restlessness, and trust The Force—Source—is always with you.

CHAPTER SIX

SELF-LOVE IS A SUPER POWER

I never knew broken hearts actually existed until Lauren dumped me (yes, the same Lauren symbolically depicted as a bird in my first mushroom ceremony!).

I met her back in college through Scotty and Nick, who belonged to the same friend group as she did at Utah State University. I was first struck by her beauty, then by how every time we hung out, we seemed to connect on a deeper level. She even tried to recruit me to work for the rival company she was employed by at one point. (I stuck with being The King at mine.)

When my dad died, Lauren showed up on my doorstep with a pie—and I didn't even know her very well at the time. It was such a thoughtful gesture that revealed her open, sweet heart. When she found herself having a crisis of faith, she confided in me. I remember telling her, "You know that it's true. Trust that you already know." I was actually trying to help her stay in the church, but my words resonated a different way.

It ended up being a pivotal moment in her life. She thought, *I do know, and I know that it's NOT true.* Our conversation sparked her to leave the Mormon faith because she trusted that her soul was speaking to her in that moment.

For years, we circled each other's lives, catching up and then losing contact again before any real relationship could blossom. One or both of us always seemed to be with someone else whenever we saw each other. The timing was never quite right.

And then, one summer night, we were hanging out together at her apartment, catching up yet again after a big chunk of time had gone by. We climbed up the fire exit to the roof and chatted under the star-filled sky. I felt like we were starring in our own romantic movie as the city skyline glittered in the distance. When we finally kissed, it was magic. I remember driving away from her house, thinking she was my dream girl.

But for whatever reason, we still never made the leap to

becoming more than friends. Life happened, and we went on leading separate but oddly connected lives. At one point, I even lived in an apartment next door to one of her best friends, and she was there visiting all the time—but neither of us even knew it.

After my June 10 experience happened, I thought, *Lauren will totally get it*, so I called her. We ended up FaceTiming. I told her the whole story, and it resonated with her. She was living in D.C. at the time but told me she was planning to be in Utah soon. I took a chance and asked her if she wanted to try MDMA with me. She enthusiastically agreed.

A few weeks later, she came to my apartment, and we had our first experience together. I remember being so excited to show her the other dimension. Of course, I didn't end up going there. I had a very standard experience versus what happened the first time at the cabin.

That night, Lauren talked my ears off for seven hours straight. I probably said three sentences the entire time, but I loved every minute of it. It seemed so healing for her to process the things that had happened in her life, and I felt lucky to be able to hold space for her.

I told her I thought we should date. She texted me later: *we'll see what the Universe has in store for us.* It was punctuated with a winky face.

When she returned to D.C., I had a very deep knowing I wanted to be with her. She was resistant to committing to anything serious. She'd just gotten out of a relationship and wasn't ready to jump right back in.

Around this same time, my company cut a deal with Best Buy and sent me to D.C. for the in-store product launch. Of all the places they could have assigned to me, I was going to be where Lauren lived. The hotel they put me up in was only five blocks away from her place. (There's that synchronicity again!)

The business part of the trip didn't go very well—no one was coming into the store, and it just felt like a waste of energy. But seeing Lauren? That was definitely well worth my time. We connected more. She opened up more. We kissed more.

One night, I was walking back to the hotel from her place. It was December and snowing lightly. I stopped to look at a sculpture in the park, and the thought hit me: *for the first time in my life, I'm in the right place, doing the right thing with the right person.* So many things had to align for me to be there—and yet, there I was.

Still, we continued our back-and-forth dance. I wanted more from her than she was ready to give. We got into a fight because I'd been clear about my intentions, and I felt like she was stringing me along. When I left town, we were back to not talking again.

That winter, I had tickets for Kaskade at the Sundance Film Festival. I was hanging out with my friends, Anna and K.D., when the date I'd planned to take with me texted that she was running an hour late. Instead of waiting for her or asking her to meet me at the concert, I did something I'd never done before: I told her we'd just meet up some other time. Then I quickly got on Facebook Marketplace and bought a third ticket that had just been posted a minute before—total synchronicity, once again!

That's how Anna, K.D., and I ended up going to the show together instead of me bringing a date to it. We were having a total blast, listening to the music and having drinks, when I felt a kick at my back. I didn't think much of it, figuring it was accidental, just someone in the crowd getting fired up and nudging me by mistake. But then there it was again. I turned around and saw none other than Lauren.

She had a huge grin on her face and gave me an even huger hug. I couldn't believe it. Now I was extra stoked I hadn't brought the date with me. We started chatting and never stopped the entire show.

Eventually, the lights came on, and the concert was over—but we still weren't done talking yet. I told K.D. and Anna to leave without me because I wanted to stay with Lauren and catch up some more. We ended up spending the rest of the night together. As always, it seemed like the Universe was trying to tell us we should be together.

A couple of days later, we got together and went on a "trip." We talked for hours and connected so deeply, it felt like we'd solved this big riddle of life. We literally kept saying to each other, "We're in on a secret." Late that night, she said the words I'd been waiting to hear for so long.

"Holy shit, I think you're my person! You're my guy! How did I miss that?" She said I'd given her unconditional love, but she'd shut me out because of her trust issues and trauma from past relationships.

We decided to be together right after that. All those amazing nudges—how she showed up when my dad died, how I gave her clarity about leaving the church, all the closeness we'd built up on our "trips" together—finally made sense. It felt like we had a soul contract nothing could break. I put my hand on her heart, told her I loved her, and felt her heart chakra blow wide open.

Her walls broke down. I was all in. She was all in. *Finally!*

For the next ninety days, we settled into a beautiful honeymoon phase. I now understood what people meant by, "When you know, you know." Lauren was *the one*. We were for sure going to get married and create a family together.

I had finally found true love, the one other person in the entire universe who got me. I remember thinking, *We are right on track for the happily ever after story.*

And then things got weird.

We were still living in different states, and I didn't hear from her for a while. I started freaking out, and we got in another fight. At the time, I was thinking, *We're just at the beginning of our relationship. We're learning. We're going to make it through this.* There was no chance in my mind that we were going to break up. But then Lauren called and said, "My soul is telling me we're not supposed to be in a romantic relationship anymore." I can still hear these words echoing in my ears as if it happened yesterday.

I was absolutely devastated. Crushed. I didn't believe it. I thought, *You told me I was your person! We're in on the secret! What are you talking about?*

I felt like a piece of my soul had been ripped away. Back when I was still a total sales bro who had gotten into this crazy, woo-woo, spiritual, psychedelic world, Lauren was the only one who understood me. She was my safe space. She truly saw me, and I saw her. To this day, I feel like a piece of Lauren lives inside me.

I became depressed to a level I didn't realize was possible.

Since I was living the startup life and had not yet gotten an investment in my business, I was low on cash—which meant I had to go back to my unfulfilling sales job. I'd just left the Mormon Church, which gutted my mother and left me unsure of why I was even on the planet, how I got here, and what happens when we die. I was missing my father and suffering in my stories.

I found myself living alone in Little Rock, Arkansas, living in a one-bedroom apartment, selling door-to-door alarm systems, exhausted and heartbroken. It was the first time in my life I experienced suicidal thoughts, which felt deeply shameful. I thought, *I only got broken up with. Why am I so weak? I need to toughen up. It's not that bad.*

One day, I was knocking on doors when I saw a red Corvette speeding down the road. All I could think was, *I hope this Corvette doesn't see me. I hope it kills me. Then I can get out of here and breathe again.* Earlier that day, I'd been in a team meeting and felt a wave of fear and sadness so big it threatened to suffocate me. I had to walk out of the room and gulp down air. Everything seemed so dark—depression, anxiety, and now panic attacks. I'd hit an all-time low. I knew I had to work on my mental state, but it wasn't like I could flip a switch and turn my depression off.

I remembered a quote from Darren Hardy, author of the *Compound Effect:* "Control what's controllable." I asked myself, *What are the things I can control to feel my best?* I started making a list:

- I can control what I eat.
- I can control if I stay hydrated.
- I can control how much sleep I get.
- I can control if I move my body.
- I can control if I journal.
- I can control if I meditate.
- I can control if I spend time out in nature.

I knew all of these things made me feel good, and I needed to mitigate as much risk as I could. I had a terrible storm going on inside my head. My goal was to calm the storm as much as possible.

I started meditating for twenty minutes, three times a day. I made sure I was getting eight hours of sleep. I ate incredibly healthfully. I spent time in nature, listening to my favorite music as the sun was coming up. I'd find a spot in the woods and journal one page every day.

I remember writing that Lauren breaking up with me was the hardest thing I'd ever gone through—even harder than my dad dying. I know it sounds crazy, but my dad didn't want to die. He loved me so much, and I felt his love. If he had the choice, he would have stayed. Lauren had seen me. She saw my soul. And she'd rejected me. Somehow, that felt worse.

Through journaling, I eventually realized I'd completely out-sourced all my happiness to her. My biggest problem wasn't that Lauren didn't love me; it was that *I didn't love myself.* I didn't think I was good enough. I'd put all of this pressure on her to make me happy, and she'd gotten overwhelmed.

DISCOVERING THE SECRET SAUCE

I remembered my new mantra: "Control what's controllable." I added a new bullet point to my list. *I can control if I love myself or not.*

I knew I couldn't risk putting my worthiness and happiness in someone else's hands ever again. I'd have to learn to love myself because then I could live a beautiful, magical, mystical, incredible, transformative life, regardless of what anyone thought about me. I'd be the master of my own life. Self-love was going to be my superpower. Once I mastered self-love, I'd be able to find a partner to share that love with.

Back when I was still searching for answers, I would meet people who were full of love and joy and think, *These guys are in on a secret.* After my heartbreak, I realized self-love was a big part of that secret.

People who love themselves can express who they are in the truest, most natural way and share their love with the intention of helping others. They're enthusiastic, engaging, and easy to be around because they don't need other people's validation. They can do the things they want to do because they're not concerned with living up to anyone else's expectations. If they fail, that's okay—it's just a learning opportunity.

People with self-love are experiencing the human experience rather than trying to fill the void. They go around radiating self-love and share it with the world. They know there's an unlimited supply of love to be spread!

I'm actually shocked at how many people don't love themselves. We are all amazing, incredible humans with gifts and talents and creativity that no one else has. Once we have self-love, life starts happening for us.

I know, easier said than done.

I started to work on developing self-love by asking myself what parts of myself I *didn't* love. Of course, the first thought to pop up was, I hate that I'm the fat kid. Ninth-grade Me especially didn't feel loved because I wanted girls to give me attention, and they didn't. Sure, I had gotten validation by being the nice guy, but deep down, I was just incredibly sad and sure my weight was the root of all my problems.

So, that summer in Arkansas, I started to write letters to ninth-grade Doug. I assured my former self, *You are enough. If you only knew what was around the corner, you wouldn't waste another moment of your life feeling anxious or sad or depressed. There's nothing wrong with you.* This small act started to heal the wounds I was still feeling, even as an adult.

Try it for yourself and see what comes up. Ask yourself, *What version of me feels unlovable? What's wrong with them? Why are they not good enough?* Start with the low-hanging fruit, like my "fat kid" story. Write younger you a letter and assure them that they are, in fact, loved and worthy and worthwhile. Continue until all your parts feel validated and welcome in your life.

Self-love doesn't happen overnight. Finding a spiritual practice—like yoga, meditation, or therapy—can help get us there. One of my best friends swears being with her crystals under the full moon gives her self-love superpowers. Whatever works. There's no right or wrong way to do it.

It doesn't matter how we get to self-love; it's just about being willing to put in the time and effort. Think of it this way: We can read every book there is about push-ups. Talk to the person who does the best push-ups in the entire world. Watch all the YouTube videos about push-ups. But if we don't actually *do* the push-ups, we're not going to get the results.

No one can do the push-ups for you.

The same goes for learning to love ourselves. We can't skip steps. We have to respect the process.

Today, I am so incredibly grateful that I had—and lost—that relationship with Lauren. She taught me how to love myself (albeit the hard way), which is such a gift. Besides, I know now that *I* was actually the one who created the magic in our relationship by letting my walls down, allowing myself to get extremely vulnerable, and giving Lauren everything I had. I put in the work, and it paid off.

It's okay that she wasn't the one because I now know the profound vulnerability required to have a deep romantic connection when the right person comes along. I also know I deserve someone who wants to be with me just as much as I want to be with them. Honestly, whoever ends up being my partner owes Lauren a thank-you card. I'm totally ready for them to come into my life because of my experience with her.

I'm always doing the work, and I am here cheering for you as you do yours. No matter where you are on your journey or how long it takes to get there, I honor and respect your effort to get better. I'm confident your hard work will pay off in the end too.

EMBRACING ALL OUR PARTS

It's so empowering to finally make peace with ourselves. Owning who we are now, along with who we used to be, validates the parts of us that used to feel unlovable. We start to embrace our differences instead of working so hard to hide them all the time.

I used to have so much shame about being the fat kid. In junior high and high school, I thought the worst possible thing ever would be if anyone saw me with my shirt off. When I got invited to my first cool kid pool party in seventh grade, I stressed about it for weeks. I almost didn't go, but a friend talked me into it. Once we got there, I said, "Hey, will you push me in the pool?" That was my way of dealing with my biggest shame: swimming with my shirt on. Hiding myself.

For years, my weight fluctuated wildly, and along with it, my self-esteem. I hit a high of 303 pounds in high school. In my early twenties, I got down to a low of 230 pounds but then gained thirty of those back almost immediately.

Every time I'd climb back on the weight-loss wagon, I'd think, *If I can just suck it up for sixty days by eating paleo and killing myself at CrossFit, I'll finally get to the finish line, where I'll be happy.* I even won a global body transformation competition at one point, earning a first-place spot in the US and third in the world. (Of course, by three months later, I'd put all the weight and then some back on again.) I absolutely suffered through it all and was miserable.

After hating my body for so long and thinking something

was wrong with it that needed to change, I had an incredible ayahuasca journey that gave me a deep respect for how beautiful my body actually is. The ceremony basically served me up a bunch of things I could take pride in when it comes to my appearance: I'm tall. I've got great hair. I get really tan. I can move. I can run. I can jump. I can experience every part of life.

I'd finally learned to love a part of myself I'd always thought was unlovable. Because I was feeling better about who I was, I started to move my body more. I actually *wanted* to eat healthy, hydrate, and sleep eight hours every night. I dropped a quick and easy forty pounds, and I wasn't forcing anything or killing myself to do it. Losing weight was just a natural byproduct of loving and respecting my body.

Today, I can even fully enjoy my favorite greasy, cheesy pizza without beating myself up over it. In the past, if someone ordered pizza, I'd think, *Okay, I'm just going to have one slice.* That always turned into three and then four and then a full pie with ice cream for dessert—and then the shame spiral would start. Now, I can have one slice and feel satisfied. It doesn't feel restrictive. I can savor the experience because I know I'm going to do it again and feel fine about it.

I look at being the former fat kid as just one part of my story now, and I can even embrace it. I also have no shame about the version of me who was a total douchebag, Mercedes-driving bro. And as much as I love yoga and meditation and ayahuasca these days, I also still love drinking beer, playing golf, and watching football. I can love all the different parts of me.

As vulnerability expert and bestselling author Brené Brown puts it: "Owning our story and loving ourselves through that process is the bravest thing we'll ever do."

We can be who we are without being ashamed. We can like seemingly opposite activities without feeling weird because our interests don't seem aligned on the surface. And we can double down on being our truest selves.

Before I learned self-love, I used to be so hard on myself. I thought I had to have a bestselling book, podcast, and $1 million and be dating an amazing girl before I would be worthy of love—even my own. Now, I can simply love the version of me that exists now.

Remember, we're never going to get this version of ourselves back. Wherever we are is always perfectly imperfect. So, don't wait for the next big thing to happen before you start loving yourself—love yourself for who you are right now, in this very moment. This version of you deserves all the love in the world too.

WHEREVER WE GO, THERE WE ARE

We can travel the whole world, but we can't hide from ourselves. Until we learn self-love, we'll always fall back on seeking other people's approval. So, I'm not overstating things when I say this is the most important work we'll ever do.

A lot of us cling to a false sense of identity: who we think we are or who someone else told us we should be. The labels we assign to ourselves—top sales rep, Mormon, my girlfriend's future husband—give us a false sense of control, and being in control makes us feel safe.

As the pandemic started to blow up, everyone scrambled to buy toilet paper—even though toilet paper clearly isn't going to stop a deadly virus, and toilet paper companies aren't going to go out of business because of it. The reason people hoarded toilet paper was that it made them feel more in control of the situation.

But when in our lives have we ever really been in full control? Never! We can control our internal state, but the external world is going to unfold the way it wants to. We can't control people, places, or things—we can only control ourselves.

We have to be brave enough to let go of the labels and identities that don't serve us anymore. When I left the Mormon church, I knew it was going to be devastating for my mom.

What I didn't anticipate was that it would also be such a big blow to my identity; I didn't know it would call who I thought I was and what I thought I knew into question. Early on in my journey, I was plagued by questions like, *How did we get here? What happens after we die? What's my purpose on Earth?* If the answers weren't what the Mormon church had taught me, what were they?

Still, I knew I had to leave to become the truest, most authentic version of me. I couldn't continue to outsource my happiness. I had to learn to sit in that discomfort and just be okay not knowing for a while. I had to trust the answers would come.

Back when I was at my lowest point, I made it a practice to ask myself what was the best thing I could do for myself just for that day. I'd listen intuitively, and then, if I achieved that, I'd consider the day a success. Sometimes, the answer was to sell a certain number of alarm systems. Others, it was like, *If I can just get out of bed and make it to lunch, that'll be a win.* I had to ask myself, *How can I win, even when I'm losing?* (Quote cred to my friend Baya!) Having a single goal to focus on helped ease the overwhelming lack of control I was feeling.

The best thing I learned from being down in that deep, dark hole was that no one was coming to save me (even though they might have wanted to). Everything I needed to get out of the situation was already inside me. I had all the tools. But the only way out of it was through it, and I was the one who had to do it.

Think of it this way: if the creator didn't want us to feel depressed or anxious or scared, we wouldn't be. There's a reason and a lesson for everything we go through. So, even though I couldn't understand at the time why the girl of my dreams—who I thought was going to be my wife and the mother of my children—would leave me, in retrospect, I can see it was because I had to learn to love myself. All that pain actually brought me an amazing gift—it made me realize what an incredible human I am and the gifts I possess.

Things aren't always going to be easy. Life is *supposed* to be hard sometimes. The most fulfilled people wouldn't take back their trials in life. Trials are just opportunities to learn. They're what teach us the most and make us better. The good news is we already have everything we need to level-up and grow.

Too often, we spend our lives doing all of these crazy things, trying not to feel a negative feeling. None of us want to feel out of control, overwhelmed, or scared, but resisting hard emotions only creates anxiety and depression. It's only when we accept those feelings and welcome them that they pass through us, and we can step into a new level of peace, enthusiasm, joy, and self-confidence.

When most of us are confronted with hard emotions, we respond by metaphorically shutting ourselves in the house, locking all the doors, turning off the lights, closing the shutters, and turning on the alarm system—yet the hard emotions continue to knock at the door. It's only when we welcome those feelings inside and sit with them that we can heal. Open the door, and let them in!

I was recently playing golf with my friends while feeling sad and anxious. Instead of following my initial instinct, which would be to try to "fix" those feelings, I realized I could be present and grateful *even though I was anxious and sad*. I could appreciate the sunny day, great friends, and a fun game while letting those hard emotions flow through me at the same time. I remembered life is not a problem to solve but an experience to be had. Keep this in mind the ✳ next time your uncomfortable emotions threaten to hijack an otherwise pleasurable experience.

I have to get better at this!

I want you to know that it's okay to feel your feelings. It's okay to be sad. It's okay to work through grief. Because wherever you go, there you are. You can't escape yourself, hard times, or hard emotions knocking at your door—but you can learn from them. Just remember they won't last forever, and there's magic on the other side.

WHAT TO DO IF YOU'RE IN THE CAVE

When I was having suicidal thoughts, it was a really intense and scary time in my life. Sadly, instead of having compassion for myself at that moment, I felt ashamed and weak. Now, I know our darkest moments are when we deserve compassion the most, especially from ourselves.

Since then, I've had my dear friend Jonny, a cousin, and several acquaintances die by suicide. They were all amazing people who are greatly missed by their family and friends. We'll never forget them or the beautiful gifts they brought to this world.

Robin Williams, Kate Spade, and Anthony Bourdain all took their own lives in the past few years too. All were absolute icons in their industry. Robin Williams was the most beloved comedian, with all the riches and fame that comes along with that designation; Kate's fashion line is adored all the world over; Anthony Bourdain hosted one of the most popular shows on television, traveling the world experiencing different cultures and eating incredible food.

Yet, all the outward fame, money, success, and adulation in the world couldn't ease their pain. That is not where happiness comes from, which these three amazing people unfortunately found out.

If you find yourself in a similar cave as I did—as my cousin, dear friend, acquaintances, Robin Williams, Kate Spade, and Anthony Bourdain did—I want you to know you are not alone. Please don't feel ashamed, weak, or beat yourself up. Whatever you do, please don't end your life.

Call a friend, family member, your therapist, or the National Suicide Prevention Lifeline at 800-273-8255 to let them know how you're feeling instead. Be gentle and compassionate with yourself. Believe me when I tell you this is the most important thing you'll ever do in regard to healing yourself.

I want you to know help is out there. *Hope* is out there. Remember, some of the best times of your life haven't even happened yet. I want you to be here to enjoy every second of them.

WE DON'T NEED ANYONE'S APPROVAL BUT OUR OWN

The best part about learning to love ourselves is that we no longer anxiously need external validation. We don't need Mom's approval. We don't need Dad's approval. We don't need our friend's approval. We can live life on our terms and not according to someone else's expectations.

Is there someone whose validation you're still seeking? If yes, why? The answer might be because acting a certain way or doing certain things is how you earned your dad's love, your boss's respect, or closeness with a friend. The problem with this equation is that it leaves out the most important person's opinion: your own.

Brené Brown tells us, "The greatest barrier to belonging is fitting in." Fitting in looks like changing who we are to get other people's validation and be accepted into a group. Belonging looks like showing up as our true selves and attracting a tribe that appreciates who we really are. Brown found the people who have the deepest sense of belonging are the ones who can stand up for what they believe in, even when that means standing alone.

What other people think of us is none of our business anyhow. As I've stated before, everyone we know creates a different version of us in their head, so we literally exist an infinite number of times in other people's minds. Trying to change who we are to satisfy their expectations of us is virtually impossible. Don't bother!

Everyone else's advice is based on their own experiences, but no one other than you knows what's best for you. The best advice you can get is the advice you give yourself.

INVITING LOVE INTO YOUR LIFE

The human experience is a spiritual experience, and love is what fuels it all. It is the one thing that connects every single person. Our natural state as humans is loving and being loved.

Once we learn to love ourselves, we no longer need the validation of others to feel happy, which gives us permission to express ourselves in the most natural way. We become explorers, living in awe and wonder as we learn and grow.

We become magnetic. People gravitate toward our energy. We meet new people, have new experiences, and grow our souls in ways we didn't know possible.

With self-love, life isn't a constant problem to be solved anymore. We don't have to race around trying to fill a void. We simply get to put our amazing skills and talents on display.

This is the secret of the super-successful: They love themselves so much, they have no problem taking risks. They see failure as a learning opportunity. They don't need anyone's approval but their own.

We already have everything we need to be wildly successful. It resides within us. We just need to go and find it. Be brave and dig deep.

Developing self-love provides us with yet another opportunity to zoom out and see that the full human experience is a spiritual experience. The whole planet turns into a canvas that we get to go experience in life. Don't waste a single second of it.

CHAPTER SEVEN

STAY CURIOUS

So, now that we've uncovered our stories…climbed out of the success void…decided to follow the white rabbit and our intuition…and finally learned to love ourselves, how can we maximize what we know?

By staying curious. Sticking to the same old thing in the same old place is exhausting and boring, like treading water. But diving into new waters is super-energizing. It wakes us up, opens the door to new ideas, and expands our minds. As former Utah football coach Urban Meyer said, "Building takes passion and energy. Maintenance is awful. It's nothing but fatigue."

Following our curiosity to new places leads to growth and progress, which in turn leads to fulfillment and inner happiness. It helps us learn to look at the world with wonder again, like a child seeing it for the first time. When we use our curiosity to develop deep-rooted passions in alignment with our unique skillset, it all combines to create a beautiful, artistic life.

After I was exposed to new paradigms and perspectives, my curiosity led me to wonder how this moment in time got here. I did a deep dive into astronomy and soon discovered there are billions upon billions of galaxies with billions and billions of stars in each of them, like I described back in Chapter One. This gave me massive cosmic perspective.

It also made me realize how special our planet is. Every incredible experience—every person who has ever lived, memory that's ever existed, and idea that's ever been imagined—happened on this tiny dot in an infinitely vast universe. Like I've said before, life existed before we were born, and it is going to continue after we leave. As humans, we're literally just passing through here.

Given our limited amount of time on Earth, our goal should be to experience everything we possibly can in life. Think of the earth like it's our own personal Disneyland. This whole planet is an amusement park, and it's just waiting for us to try new things.

HOW CAN A UTAH NATIVE NOT KNOW HOW TO SKI?

Even though I grew up in Salt Lake City, home to some of the best ski mountains in the country, I'd never tried skiing until a few years ago. All of my friends already knew how to ski, and I was afraid of looking like a fool. Besides, I didn't even know how to rent skis and was too embarrassed to ask.

One of my favorite quotes is, "Fear is the precursor to courage," so I finally mustered up the courage to take my first skiing lesson at Deer Valley. The class consisted of me—a six-foot-four, 220-pound grown man—and three third-graders. Learning how to "pizza" and "hot dog" on the bunny hill with a bunch of little kids was nerve-wracking. Even my ski instructor was younger than I was!

Every time I fell, I wondered what other people were thinking about me. And then I had an *aha!* moment—I realized nobody cared what I was doing. Everyone was caught up in their own world. It was such a huge weight off of my shoulders.

After a few more lessons, skiing became one of my favorite hobbies. For years, I'd let fear stop me from pursuing this beautiful new activity that is endlessly entertaining and social. I'm so grateful I pushed past my fear.

The newest skill I'm honing these days is golf. Utah has top-notch golf courses, but I was always ashamed of not being able to play well enough to keep up with the other players. The few times I tried, I'd swing as hard as I could and the ball would only go three feet. It was so embarrassing. Then, I hired a coach, learned the basics, and discovered a new passion for the game. I'm still not an expert, but now I can enjoy playing a round with my friends and do it every chance I get.

All it took was finding out that no one cares if I'm a beginner. Nobody is looking, laughing, or pointing and staring at me. No one gives a shit. People actually think it's admirable I'm willing to try something new. My friends support and encourage me. They share tips and tricks. They buy into my excitement and cheer me on.

THE IMPORTANCE OF "I DON'T KNOW"

How many times have you been in a conversation where someone brings up a subject you have no idea about, but you don't want ask questions because you feel stupid?

There's a lot of power in the words *I don't know*. Instead of making us sound dumb or uneducated, saying, "I don't know" does the opposite. It actually earns respect from others, builds trust, and empowers us to learn more. When we're willing to let our guard down and be vulnerable, it shows that we're open to learning a new angle.

Besides, it's okay not to know! No one expects us to know everything. I didn't know how to ski. I didn't know how to golf. I didn't know how to build an app. I went and did all those things anyway, asking questions and seeking guidance along the way.

If there weren't new things to learn and challenges to overcome, life would be so boring. Start to see what you don't know—yet—as an opportunity to expand your knowledge and experiences.

ALWAYS SAY YES TO EXPERIENCES

I grew up in an upper-middle-class neighborhood where a lot of successful people lived. Two neighbors in particular, Dave Ayre and Stan Hansen, both took me under their wing and became mentors to me in my teens.

I'll never forget sitting in Dave's office one day and asking him, "What piece of advice would you want to instill in a sixteen-year-old like me?"

He told me, "Money will come and go. Things will come and go. But you always need to say yes to and pay for experiences. If you have the choice between buying a new car or spending the same amount of money going on three trips around the world, go on the trips."

His advice has stuck with me all these years.

Back in college, I had an opportunity to do a service project in Nepal. My initial thought was, *I don't really have any desire to do that.* But Dave's advice echoed through my head. I went and now have such fond memories of serving the Nepalese people. That experience truly enhanced the quality of my life.

Another example: my friend Rosie recently invited me to a cooking class. I'm by no means a chef or even remotely good in the kitchen. I didn't even think I was interested in learning. Once again, I immediately thought of Dave's advice, went to the class, and now, I actually love cooking.

Especially when it comes to people we love, always say yes to the experience. Relationships may change and people will die, but a special moment in time with them lasts forever. There's no price tag we can put on that.

EXPERIENCING THE WORLD OF WOO-WOO

Once I decided the Mormon church didn't feel true to me, I decided to head out into the world in search of the truth. I wanted to talk to anyone who seemed like they might have some insight and experience everything that might lead me to it. I ended up spending $100,000 and the better part of five years doing just that. I tried (and this is by no means an exhaustive list):

- Crystals
- Astrology
- Psychics
- Reiki
- Ecstatic dance
- EMDR
- Silent meditation retreats in the mountains
- Yoga retreats in the US, Costa Rica, and Bali
- Sound bath work
- Cryotherapy
- Bulletproof and biohacking
- Holotropic breathwork
- Wim Hof Method
- Neurotherapy
- Fireside camps at Burning Man
- So. Many. Psychedelics.
- Flow camp in the mountains of Utah and California
- Hiring both a personal meditation coach and a spiritual coach
- Tarot cards

I'm not sure most of it got me any closer to the truth, but I kept following my curiosity. Everything was new and exciting. It was electrifying, it lit me up, and I'll always have great memories of the experiences I had while I was out there searching.

There's so much bullshit in the spiritual space, but there's also a lot of good stuff. It's really just a matter of what resonates. For me, crystals don't really do it. Astrology doesn't seem to add to my experience. I don't see psychics anymore, and reiki did nothing for me.

Ecstatic dance wasn't my jam (although some people swear by it). The same goes for EMDR—eye movement desensitization and reprocessing—where they flash lights on the sides of the eyes to trigger stored memories of trauma. But silent retreats were great and sound baths were especially nice when I was in pain, like after Lauren broke up with me.

Yoga (especially in Bali) is totally my thing. I still do cryotherapy, a bit of biohacking, and bulletproof. I enjoy holotropic breathwork and Wim Hoff Method on occasion. Changing our breathing patterns can have a very powerful effect on the body. We can basically create a psychedelic trip in our brains by altering the carbon monoxide levels in our blood! And there's nothing more illuminating than sitting around a fire with like-minded people at Burning Man.

Neurotherapy was also really cool. After my first MDMA trip where I felt like I'd literally been handed the keys to the universe, I was more than a little freaked out by what had happened to my brain, so I started working with a neurotherapist. I would go see her twice a week and put on a cap with electrodes designed to read my brainwaves. By listening to certain tones and playing a brain puzzle she had me watch on a screen, my brainwaves would get calmer, and as a result, I would feel calmer.

PSYCHEDELICS ARE IT

But no question about it, psychedelics—especially aya-huasca—are what spoke most deeply to me. I truly believe taking psychedelics is the most profound experience we can have as humans. They really show you your subconscious personal blocks—like my long-buried trauma, like my child-hood sexual abuse. They can also connect us so deeply to another person, like I experienced with Lauren.

When I told my neurotherapist I was going to try aya-huasca for the first time, she was really intrigued. She completed a full brain scan on me both before and after I did it, and she couldn't believe the results. She said it looked like the scans came from two entirely different brains and told me, "What happened to your brain in one weekend would take me twenty years of work with a patient."

She sent my report off to her mentor because she felt it con-tained such unbelievable data. She even said she could see the change in me the second I walked in the room. There was a lightness, engaged energy, and a softness to me that hadn't been there before. Finding ayahuasca has been such a game-changer in my life.

When I went to my second Flow Camp—which was pretty cool too—I connected with a friend of a friend named Mary who is a shaman for 5-MeO-DMT, a psychedelic better known as the "God molecule." I'd always been scared to try it before this, but I trusted Mary. I told her, "I've been waiting for you."

She had me lie on a bed while she put on a headdress, began chanting and praying, and pulled tarot cards. She told me, "If the thought even occurs to you that you want to take more while you're doing this, don't contemplate or wrestle with it. Just do it."

Once I inhaled the 5-MeO-DMT, I fell into a void where nothing existed—it was just pure black. I didn't even know who Doug was anymore or that I'd ever had a life on Earth. Then, I heard a little whistle and realized it was me breathing out smoke. At that moment, I felt like I could reach my arms across the entire universe. My entire essence *became* the universe, I was so massive and expansive.

I smoked some more. This time, it was like I got shot out of a cannon. I ripped through reality, and I was swimming in infinity with God. My soul dissolved back into the oneness of being home in the universal consciousness. I was finally able to grasp, understand, and feel the essence of infinity and felt the united whole that we truly are all one!

Now, that was the kind of truth I'd been seeking for five long years!

I looked at Mary and started laughing. "No way! Our entire human existence is an atom in a water molecule in an infinite ocean bigger than anyone could ever possibly imagine." She just nodded and smiled back at me. Yup. I finally got it.

That trip made me realize the things I took so seriously—the girl who didn't text me back, that person who was rude to me—are so minuscule and insignificant compared to our place in the cosmos. I left feeling super-stoked about life, knowing that everything we do is just part of the experience.

Like I said before, I rarely do psychedelics these days, and when I do, it is very carefully. But the experiences I had with them have been truly instructive, therapeutic, and life-altering. The effects will stay with me for a lifetime.

TAKE THE CHALLENGE

So, let's go do all the things. Let's learn to ski, play golf, and cook. Let's eat all the food and jump in the ocean and go skinny dipping. Let's see how we can bring our gifts to the world. Because at the end of the day, it's just a big cosmic joke—and now we're all in on it.

Here's my challenge to you. Try something new this week

that you've always wanted to do but didn't because you were afraid of failing or what other people might think about you. Maybe it's something like:

- Gardening
- Pottery
- Cooking
- Skiing
- Golf
- Speaking a new language
- Learning how to code
- Writing a book
- Playing an instrument
- Running a marathon

Go to a different workout class, hike a new trail, visit the animal shelter, or foster a pet. Don't go to the workout class because subconsciously you feel you need a six-pack to be lovable; do it to respect and appreciate your body. Do it because you can run and jump and be strong. Do it because you're human and you get to experience life. Follow your soul's urge, set your own path, and do what lights you up.

If there's still some lingering fear hanging around, remember that every professional—everyone who is now incredible at what they do—sucked at the beginning. I want you to have the courage to suck at something new too. If you were a virtuoso at it immediately, what kind of challenge would that be? You're not *supposed* to be good at something you've never done before.

Besides, who cares what other people think, anyway? We have to stop asking people who have never been where we're going for directions. We don't need their external validation or permission anymore.

There will never be a perfect time to start, and you're never going to be fully ready. It's time to realize you're not a perfectionist; you're just scared. That's okay. Do it anyway.

There's always going to be a mountain to climb. No one is coming to save you, so embrace the challenge. Trials are just another opportunity to grow.

Stay curious. Go explore. And always say yes to the experience.

CHAPTER EIGHT

MOVEMENT IS LIFE

In *World War Z,* there's a deadly pandemic turning people into zombies. As the movie kicks off, Brad Pitt's character and his family are running through the streets of Philadelphia trying to get away from them. They take a turn into an apartment complex, where a kind, non-zombified family lets them in and gives them some food.

They discuss what to do next. The other family believes it's best to hunker down, wait for the storm to pass, and then make a decision. Brad's character disagrees, saying, "Movement is life."

Brad and his family decide to take off and end up surviving. The family that stayed still—waiting the zombie apocalypse out in their apartment—met a quick zombie death.

I love this movie because it reminds me that when we stay in the same place—even though it's comfortable—it can be the death of our growth and advancement as a human being. Even if we're scared, we have to keep going. Even if it's risky and we don't understand, it's important to keep moving forward in our lives.

FOCUS ON THE ACTION, NOT THE END GAME

I was at a point in my life where I was making big changes, shedding old versions of myself, doing personal work, and having spiritual experiences that completely changed my paradigm. I'd left the company where I was known as The King and was feeling empowered enough to leave Salt Lake for somewhere new. I started asking myself, *Where would be a new cool place to live?*

Austin, LA, and New York were all in the running. But my twin sister Denise and another friend had just moved to New York City, which eventually pushed it to the top of the list. I had a newfound self-confidence, so I wasn't intimidated by the big city like I might have been in the past. I visited several times, had a blast, and actually even found an apartment that I liked in my price range. For whatever reason, though, I knew intuitively to hold off on signing the lease.

Around this same time, I went to my second Flow Camp. That's where I met Mary, the 5-MeO-DMT shaman who led me through both my experiences with the "God molecule." After my first, more positive trip with the medicine, we met at a café the morning after to do an integration session—basically, to talk about what I'd learned and put it into a context that could be useful in my life.

As we were chatting, a gentleman leaned in and said, "I'm so sorry to interrupt you, but are you talking about psychedelics?" We said we were, and he asked to listen in on our conversation because he had a strong interest in the topic. We agreed.

After Mary left, this guy and I continued chatting. He asked about my background, what I was doing at Flow Camp, and what my ultimate goals were. He seemed fascinated by my answers, especially about how I was trying to raise consciousness for people who needed it the most. I showed him my beta version of my app, and he asked to stay in contact. I still didn't know much about him but agreed. He was a nice enough guy.

GET YOURSELF A HYPE FRIEND

Baya is my hype friend, and I'm hers. Everyone needs a hype friend—someone who cheers you on in absolutely everything you do in life. If you don't have one yet, start looking for one. It can be life-changing!

Around the time I was deciding where to move, Baya got

asked to speak at SXSW in Austin. I immediately bought a ticket to go see her talk. Right before I was leaving, I got an email from Khotso—the gentleman I met at Flow Camp who listened in on my integration session with Mary—saying he'd looked over my business and app and wanted to talk more. Although he hadn't shared with me what he did for work, it turned out he was a part of an accelerator fund that invested in conscious entrepreneurs.

I recognized his area code as being in Austin, so I emailed him back saying I'd be in the area the next day. We arranged to have dinner together.

I didn't even check into my hotel before going to meet Khotso. He told me his company was looking for an entrepreneur actively working to raise consciousness and make a difference in the world. I fit the bill perfectly. At the time, I still only had a beta version of The Daily Shifts, so he asked how much money I'd need to launch my app. I told him $500,000. He agreed to give it to me on the condition I moved to Austin.

It became clear in that moment why I hadn't signed the lease on the New York apartment. I immediately said, "Let's do it." We shook hands on it, and that was that. Khotso's company would provide me with a half a million dollars, and I was relocating to Austin.

I went to Baya's event, and of course, she was amazing. I had the most incredible weekend, meeting all these new friends and getting plugged into a network right away. I was feeling the flow of Austin and watching life unfold in front of me.

FOLLOWING MY INTUITION TO A NEW ADVENTURE

The initial six-figure investment from my mentors at my former company was going fast. What I'd initially envisioned as being only an app had now morphed into an app, an online course, an e-book, a weekly video challenge, a newsletter, and an active social media presence. Khotso's half a million couldn't come fast enough.

Once I was in Austin, though, his group kept pushing out the date of their investment. First by thirty days, then sixty, then more. They told me they had more pressing financial dealings to address before they'd have any money available for me. I was assured that the group still wanted to invest in me and loved my idea, but they just needed a little more time.

Ninety more days passed without any movement, and money was getting tight. I had only $7,000 left to my name and was not even bringing in enough income to cover my monthly personal and business expenses. I'd never stressed about money before, but I was certainly starting to. I learned a valuable lesson: it's not a done deal until the money's in your bank account.

Around the same time, I came across an ad from Gerard Adams, the founder of *Elite Daily*, who later sold the online news platform for $50 million after he got into plant medicine and spirituality. I clicked on it and learned he was forming a mastermind group for conscious entrepreneurs. I thought it looked interesting, so I set up a phone call with his team.

I loved everything I was hearing about the group and how they could help me build my personal brand. It sounded like exactly what my business needed. But the five-day retreat alone cost $5,000. There was no way I could attend.

But after meditating on it, I couldn't deny the message my soul was sending me. I had to go to the mastermind, never mind my financial difficulties. So, I decided to trust the Universe. I called back and signed myself up. Including the flight and hotel, I was left with $800 to my name.

Right before I was about to leave for the mastermind, Khot-so's group called me in and told me they had an incredible offer for me. They wanted to buy my entire company out for $1.3 million, including a contract paying me a salary of $200,000 a year for the next four years. There was only one catch: they were going to rebrand The Daily Shifts as their own app, and I would be working for them. The Daily Shifts as I knew it would be dead.

I could have grabbed that $1.3 million and clung to it like a life raft. My bank account was almost totally drained. But it was still the easiest no I've ever given. I didn't even consider the deal or take a day to debate it. I just knew it wasn't right, and there was something better out there for me if I trusted my gut.

When I look back at this moment, I like to view it from a bird's eye perspective. There I was, with not even $1,000 to my name, turning down a seven-figure offer. Why? I can't explain it. I just knew the Universe had bigger plans for me.

So, I declined right then and flew directly to LA for the mastermind. My first night there, I had to walk home from dinner because I couldn't afford a Lyft. I'd been balling out at my former company, and now, here I was, basically broke. I called my buddy JT and burst out laughing. He laughed along with me and told me to keep believing in my brand.

I could have been so anxious at that moment. But unless we're running away from a tiger or a bear, anxiety never does us any good. No amount of anxiety can change the outcome of a situation, so I turned it into a funny moment with a friend instead.

In the weekly calls leading up to the actual event, I was always more of a behind-the-scenes kind of guy—probably because I didn't want to be vulnerable and put myself out there. But at the mastermind, Gerard convinced me I needed to be up front and center, and also, that part of my business offering should be taking on private clients. I spent the rest of my time there mapping out what my coaching program would look like.

I'd only been home for three days when a former colleague from my old job reached out. He said he'd seen me change, that it seemed like I'd really found out who I was, and he wanted to affect the same kind of change in his own life. I told him about my coaching program, and he signed up for it immediately. That meant I'd already recouped the full $5,000 I spent on the mastermind.

The following week, the same thing happened again with another former colleague. Ten days after returning from the mastermind, I'd already received $10,000 from my investment. The Universe always responds to effort!

I think the biggest misconception surrounding the Law of Attraction is that whatever you think will come true—that if your thoughts are in alignment, you'll automatically receive whatever it is that you're seeking. But the truth is, you actually have to go out and do the work. Remember: *no one can do the push-ups for you.*

You can't just wish for somebody to get you a bike and expect it to land on your doorstep tied up in a pretty red bow. You have to put yourself in situations to succeed—for example, go to biking events or get up the courage to ask someone for their bike (or in my case, build an app by maxing out my credit cards not knowing how or when my investment in my dream would pay off). Sitting at home won't get you anything.

When I was down to my last $800 in the world, I followed my intuition and was rewarded for it. It was actually fun waiting to see how everything would shake out. And I knew it would be fine because I went out and did the work.

(MOST) ANXIETY IS FUTURE-BASED AND FICTIONAL

Don't let anxiety stand in the way of moving forward toward your goals.

There are two reasons why we get anxious: there's something we desperately want, and we're afraid we're not going to get it, or there's something we already have, and we're scared we're going to lose it. It's that simple: there's something we don't want to happen, and we're afraid it will; there's something we want to happen, and we're scared it won't.

The thing to remember here, though, is that neither of those scenarios are happening right now. They're future-based and fictional. Especially when we're thinking six months out, nine months out, a few years out, there are so many things that can happen that we can't possibly predict. No amount of anxiety can control what is going to happen or how things will turn out.

Because we don't want to feel our anxiety, we resist it, and it starts to spiral. The longer we resist uncomfortable emotions, the more they persist. *Whatever you resist, persists.* Relax into the emotions instead, let them move through you, and eventually, they will pass.

The more aligned we become with our purpose, the more anxiety, fear, and doubt creeps in. This is natural. One doesn't come without the other. Lean into it anyhow.

Untie yourself from what you think is supposed to be happening in your life. The true definition of suffering is getting attached to any specific outcome. Embrace what *is* happening, not what you want in some far-off future. You have everything you need, right now, in this moment, and the Universe knows what it's doing.

Remember, though: you can't skip the steps. No one can do the push-ups for you. As author Joseph Campbell once said, "The cave you fear to enter holds the treasure you seek." Go into that scary place, and free yourself from everything that's been holding you back.

Just a note that clinical depression and anxiety are chemical imbalances and real disorders. The messages in this book can be great adjunct therapy and medications, but it's important to seek professional care whenever necessary.

JUST KEEP SWIMMING

Great white and mako sharks have to keep moving in order to produce oxygen for their bodies. No movement equals no oxygen equals death. And so, they keep on swimming.

As humans, we have to remember to always keep going too. Movement brings new experiences, skills, and people into our orbit. Keep going.

Even when things aren't looking good. Even though it looks like there's no way it's going to work out. Even when you don't have any answers. Be willing to put yourself out there because the Universe always responds to effort.

Movement is life, so keep moving.

CHAPTER NINE

MEET YOUR HIGHEST SELF

I've dropped the name Casey Baugh more than once in this book. That's not only because he's been an amazing mentor to me. It's also because there's so much to admire about him.

Casey has so much financial wealth and, in my opinion, is the epitome of business success, but it's his *personal* wealth that's so enticing to me. He has a beautiful family and home. He's well-respected and a wonderful friend and gives back to the community. He's in great shape. I've never seen him get angry or upset, which makes him a joy to be around. The guy is basically a human magnet—he draws everyone to him.

I recently went golfing with Casey to celebrate a big buyout of one of his companies, and I asked him what he thought his superpower was. I was trying to define what makes him different from so many other people I know. His answer, unsurprisingly, had nothing to do with his phenomenal sales skills, his ability to spot a killer investment, or being an expert networker.

He simply said, "I've always loved where I was. I loved being a salesperson, and then I loved being an assistant manager and manager, and then I loved being a VP. I loved when we were growing the business, when we became a hundred-million-dollar company, and then when we were an eight-billion-dollar company. I loved when I first met my wife Chelsea, and then we were poor newlyweds, and then when we had our kids. I wasn't ever waiting to be happy—I was just happy now."

Be happy where you are and NOW!

It was such a profound and beautiful thing to hear. Casey's superpower turned out to be self-love multiplied by his incredible ability to always live in the moment. Now, that's a great goal to have and an even better one to achieve.

As Khotso and I always used to say, "This is it! Right now! This is life! We're doing it!" Life is never *not* right now, so enjoy every minute of it. (Yes, Khotso and I remained friends even after I turned down his offer to rebrand The Daily Shifts. Our mantra means even more to me today because Khotso died in a tragic accident in 2020. The way his life ended so unexpectedly only highlights why it's so important to live in the moment.)

WHATEVER YOU DO, DO THE WORK

When it comes to self-development, the way we get there doesn't matter. I tried a whole list of things before I found what worked best for me. The best path for you is whatever resonates the most. Whatever you do to work on yourself with the intention of bettering yourself, I honor and respect that.

Once you start getting in alignment, healing past stories, and tapping into your talents, part of the process is having a lot of anxiety, fear, and doubt come up. Whenever that happens, try to remember that pressure is a privilege. People who aren't doing anything big with their lives don't ever experience pressure because they're playing small. That's not you.

We don't go to the movies to see regular ordinary people having ordinary lives; we go to see superheroes doing incredible things and taking massive risks. Like I told ninth-grade Doug in the letters I wrote when I was working on healing my "fat kid" story, if you truly knew what the Universe had in store for you and how your life was going to turn out, you wouldn't spend any more time worrying about it.

How you feel is no one else's fault. It takes just as much energy to complain and feel negative as it does to actually do the work. Be sure to spend that energy doing something that will foster positive growth—even if it's uncomfortable.

The truth is, it's going to be uncomfortable either way. We

can either sink down into our discomfort by trying to mask and avoid it, or we can go do the work and find freedom on the other side. Pursuing things that make us grow might give us a little more pain upfront, but there's also the promise of relief on the backend. And we're going to do the work eventually anyhow, whether we do it in an hour or when we can't stand the pain of staying the same anymore.

So, take a risk. The Universe always has our back. The future will be better than we can imagine. And every moment is better off because we've interacted with it.

KUNDALINI DOESN'T PAY THE RENT

When people first get into personal development work, spirituality is an amazing new frontier, and they want to explore everything, all at once. They get obsessed with how they can get better and what else they can do. Pretty soon, they find themselves stuck in an endless circle of "What's next?".

The purpose of personal development is to live a beautiful human life, not to get sucked down a New Age rabbit hole. That's really just procrastinating, putting off doing the real work. Don't use seeking out new practices and methods as an excuse to stop doing everything else in life.

As I always like to say, your Kundalini practice may be amazing, and it truly is an incredible tool for healing and connection, but you still have to pay the rent. We have to provide value in the world, so we can be compensated with money, so we can pay for the necessities of living. That's the reality of the world we live in.

Stay in balance. Do the work, but don't let it overshadow everything else.

DREAM WILDLY

Sit back, close your eyes, and think about your wildest dreams.

What does your family and marriage look like? Where do you live? How is the view? What does your house look like? How is it furnished?

Take it a step further. Who are your friends? Maybe you're hanging out with Barack Obama, Brené Brown, Carl Sagan, and Oprah Winfrey. You're all part of your special book club and get together every weekend.

Now, go even further. What have you accomplished in your personal and professional life? Is your book a number-one *New York Times* bestseller? Are you traveling the world, speaking and inspiring people? Did your side hustle blow up and make you hundreds of millions of dollars? Are you able to give back to your favorite charitable cause now because of your wild financial success?

Great!

Now, imagine all of your wishes are fulfilled. Every single dream you ever had came true. You have everything you've ever wanted and more.

Now, ask yourself: *how would I treat the girl taking my order at the coffee shop*? If you're like most people, you'd probably be incredibly nice and patient with her. You'd be sweet and smile. You'd make small talk, tip her generously, and thank her. When you have everything you could ever want, it's easy to be kind to others, right?

Well, that's the energy every single one of us needs to take into the world every day. Starting now. We need to show up as the version of ourselves that already has all of our wishes fulfilled. We have to embody the emotion of an abundant life to attract it into our lives.

My spiritual teacher Biet Simkin and I were talking awhile back, and she asked me to imagine my perfect partner. I described someone inspiring, who helped me grow, and was supportive and creative. She told me, "That person already exists. But you're showing up in the world as depressed and mopey at the moment, so she's going to miss you. She isn't going to be attracted to you because your energy isn't at the right frequency right now." She was so spot on with this revelation!

And it's not only true in the dating world, it's true with everything. We need to make every person, situation, and experience we encounter better off because we interacted with it. We need to start acting like the people we want to become and invite our dreams into reality.

START WHERE YOU ARE

No matter where you find yourself right now, you can have an incredible, beautiful, magical life.

Remember my friend Charles, a homeless heroin addict? Charles who used to overdraft his bank card every week just to fill up his car with gas to get to work? Well, now, he's completely clean and sober, has a beautiful wife and two kids, and works with the top business people in Utah. In fact, he's working on a project right now that's going to have a profound impact on the community he lives in. He changed his life dramatically, and so can you.

Many people feel they are not everything they could be yet. That's okay. Just start taking small, simple steps. Trust that something bigger than you is guiding you. Know and truly believe that anything is possible, every moment is better off because you interacted with it, and always remember that some of the best days of your life haven't even happened yet.

THE PATH IS UNPREDICTABLE—JUST KEEP GOING!

Even though it's important to have goals, the actual way we get there is often completely unpredictable. Oftentimes, we can't make sense of things except when we're looking back at them. Life is always happening for us, and the Universe has our best interests in mind.

THE RISE AND FALL OF AN UNLIKELY FOOTBALL STAR

When I was in high school, I always wanted to be popular. I wanted to be cool. I wanted validation that would free me from my "fat kid" story. What I actually was: a nice kid who was trying to be popular and cool (and not fat).

I played on the football team, and by sophomore and junior year, I wasn't a superstar by any means. I was just okay. The team, though, was insanely good—we were nationally ranked, and our quarterback and star running back were being recruited by every major college. Multiple teammates ended up playing at the top division one schools, and one even went on to play in the NFL.

I saw those guys getting recognition and often wished my name could be in the paper alongside them. Getting recruited seemed like the ultimate accomplishment. I dreamed of being a popular football star, but the truth was, I just wasn't that good. It was cool to be part of the team, but I hated practice, conditioning, and getting beat up by guys who were way better than me.

My junior year, I was third-string offensive lineman for most of the season. We were favored to win the state championship, but I was so low on the depth chart, the probability of me getting into the big game was close to nil.

And then, just before our last few games, something finally clicked in me. I decided, *I'm going to stop resisting everything. I'm just going to go out there and have fun.* I got into an excellent flow for the first time in my life. I started practicing harder, having a better time with it, and playing better as a result.

Right before the playoffs, the two guys in front of me suffered season-ending injuries, and our star offensive lineman broke his leg. I literally went from last in a line of talented players to starting in the semi-final game. All of a sudden, the team was really relying on me.

A dad of a senior player called me before that game and said, "We just want you to know we're all cheering for you." I got the underlying message: don't mess this up. I understood everyone was nervous because the best players were out, and I was the one taking their place.

I ended up playing an awesome game at the University of

Utah stadium under the lights. There was a lot of press there, big energy going on, and yet, somehow, I never felt panicked. I just dropped into a flow state and was super happy. I didn't feel the pressure. I was just excited—and I didn't screw up one time.

The game came so easily. I absolutely dominated my competition. I was totally out of my head, in the flow, just reacting. Although we ended up getting upset by our opponent, I can still remember walking away from that stadium feeling super happy with my performance. Even *I* didn't know I could be that good.

After that, the coach pulled me in and said, "Your game film is incredible. You actually might be able to play college football." I'd graded out at a 100 percent in the last game—better than every other offensive lineman.

Earlier in the season, I'd been just this scrub, and now, I had a chance of being recruited. It was what I always wanted. I had excellent grades, so I started talking to all the Ivy league schools: Penn, Cornell, Dartmouth. I even got nominated to be captain of the football team the next year.

Now that I wasn't just another guy on the sidelines, I started taking football—and my life—much more seriously. It showed in the way I acted on the field, in the classroom, and with my friend group. I ran for student body vice president and won. I'd never been great at basketball before then, and in a summer tournament in Las Vegas, I scored forty points in a single game. I was just in an incredible flow. I even started to get attention for basketball too.

And then, the summer before my senior year, I started feeling really sick. I was always jittery and sweating. I lost all my speed, not to mention thirty-seven pounds in a single month. I didn't understand what was going on.

Still, I flew to Philly to do a workout with the University of Pennsylvania. I undeniably sucked. My strength was off. My speed was off. I didn't perform at all. The coach who was recruiting me gave me a disappointed, "You looked a lot different on film." Let's just say it was not my finest moment.

I got to my first padded football practice of the season and was similarly not on my game. I—the new captain of the team—was completely underperforming and getting totally beat up. And then I passed out.

I went to the doctor, who did some scans and told me he was concerned I had a hole in my heart. If that was true, I'd never be able to ever play sports again. It turned out to be a misdiagnosis, thankfully.

Then, he ran some blood work, which showed I had Graves'

Disease—aka, hyperthyroidism. It is insanely rare for someone in my age bracket. I was told I could have my thyroid removed or take medication for the rest of my life. Those were my only options.

The coach toned back my exercise. I missed the first three games of the season. I had to take pills. I needed to gain the weight I'd lost and did it in the most unhealthy way possible. I wasn't strong. I wasn't mobile. I just wasn't the same.

Six weeks later, I went in to do more labs. The doctor was in shock. He told me I didn't have Graves' Disease anymore. He'd never seen anything like it. I literally haven't taken medication since.

The *Deseret News*—a big paper in Utah—sent a writer to interview me. I thought it would be a little article, hidden in the back of the sports section, but when I opened the paper to read it, I was shocked to see my picture on the front page! It was another dream come true—although not exactly the way I'd envisioned it. The story centered on my diagnosis of Graves' Disease and how it had affected my play.

I had what you'd call a pretty mediocre senior football season, and as a result, I lost a lot of interest from the college football teams. Most of them just kind of stopped talking to me. By the end, only Cornell was still in the mix. They let me know there was one player higher on their list, but they were expecting him to take a spot that had been offered to him at Yale. If that turned out to be the case, the spot was mine.

By this point, I wasn't even sure playing football was what I was meant to do. I remember praying to God to make my decision as clear as possible.

The next day, the coach called and said the other guy had taken the spot. I thought, *Well, there's my answer right there.* My high school coach found a spot for me on the team at Kenyon College, but I just remember thinking, *I know I'm not supposed to play.* I turned it down and walked away from football.

I'd had my moment of fame. I started in the playoffs for the best team. I got recruited. I made it in the newspaper. And then, the Universe gave me Graves' Disease, cured it, and made it very simple for me not to play college football. Looking back, it's like the Universe had different plans for me.

Like I said, you can't predict the path. I could have never known how this whole story was going to go, but it was such a gift. The Universe showed true grace for me in that experience. It forced me to look at my life differently and threw me into a leadership role. That actually paid off big time—it was prepping me to become the truest version of myself.

If I'd gone to Cornell, my entire life would have been different. I would have never been The King of door-to-door sales. I would've never found Casey Baugh. I'd never start The Daily Shifts. And I wouldn't be telling you any of this right now.

FROM CONFERENCE ATTENDEE TO MAIN STAGE SPEAKER

Here's another example: in 2017, I felt inspired to go to the 10X Growth Conference because there was such an incredible lineup of speakers. I went by myself and enjoyed them all. At one point, I felt a massive rush of energy, accompanied by a knowing that I was going to be onstage one day. I could see it all so clearly in my head.

Over the next four years, this vision came with me on an incredible journey, complete with moments where I had to walk home because I couldn't even afford a Lyft. I knew everything was going to work out because I was on the right path. I was open and in integrity. And I was putting in the work, not just sitting home and trying to manifest and expecting the life I wanted and all that came with it to just show up at my door. I was moving forward.

A few months ago, I was driving home, and the thought popped into my head to reach out to a former friendly rival from my old company, Sam Taggart. We were always competing to be top sales rep back in the day. Since he'd left the firm, Sam had gone on to found a successful consulting company called D2D Experts, and he puts on an annual conference, D2DCON.

Following my own advice of always listening to the nudges and whispers of the Universe, I gave Sam a call and invited him to a yoga class. Afterward, we grabbed dinner together. Sam opened up about some intimate parts of his life, and I realized he was going through a spiritual awakening. I told him, "I've been there. I've walked this path." I gave him some insights about how to tap in, surrender, and learn to love himself.

He appreciated my input and asked me about my company. I told him about my e-book, online courses, eighty-page workbook, masterclasses, and coaching practice with students. Sam was very enthusiastic about all the work I'd done. He said he thought the door-to-door industry really needed to hear my message and invited me to speak at D2DCON. (Actually, he asked me to be a headliner!)

"Do you have a speech prepared?" he asked.

Why, yes, as a matter of fact I did. Two months earlier, I'd had a strong intuition to hire Dorothy, who I met at the Gerard Adams mastermind the year before, to help create a new webinar for me. It basically contained the entire talk I wanted to give at D2DCON, and lucky for me, I'd already been practicing it daily in anticipation of doing the webinar. I was completely prepared and on my game.

When I saw the schedule of speakers for the event, it was the most beautiful moment. Three of the people I'd be sharing the stage with were the same huge names I'd gone to see at 10X Growth Conference four years earlier. And I was the only one of us invited to speak twice, both days of the event.

I was in the green room getting mic'd up, when I found myself having a conversation with famed author, leadership speaker, and pastor John C. Maxwell. I told him I admired his work, and he listened with interest about mine. I couldn't believe I was rubbing shoulders with these top high-performers.

It was a huge thrill to be on that stage I'd envisioned four years ago. The audience seemed really engaged and invested in what I had to say. But the best part came when thirty-one people signed up for my coaching program after my talk. Two weeks before, I didn't even know I was going to be a headline speaker for an important industry conference, and now, I'd closed a multiple six-figure deal on that stage.

I had all this work prepared for Sam because I'd followed the breadcrumbs every step of the way. I built an app. I created a course. I hired Dorothy. I surrendered to not knowing how it was going to unfold.

Along with self-love, I guess my other superpower is when I'm standing at the ledge, I'll always jump off when the Universe is telling me to jump. I don't know how I'm going to land, where I'm going to land, or how it's going to unfold—but since I'm committed to the higher path and living in integrity, I always trust I'll be taken care of and things will end up more beautiful than I could have imagined. I know this is just the beginning of a whole new chapter in my life.

LISTEN AND LEARN

In the movie *Life Itself*, the main character writes a thesis about how we are all such unreliable narrators in our own lives. We're basically wrong about everything, so we need to stop trying to figure it out.

Through several generations, the movie shows how we all have these moments where—even though we have our own plans—things take a different turn. Something happens to completely change the course of our lives that we never could have anticipated. The traumatic events depicted in the braided storyline all sync up in the end, and those experiences are what allow two strangers to cross paths, fall in love, and create something new and beautiful. It's all an intertwined web of beautiful synchronicity.

Similarly, while our own personal twists of fate may seem cruel at the time, somehow in the end, everything turns out just like it was supposed to be. Like how I had plans of playing football in college, but then I got Graves' Disease. Although it seemed pretty terrible in the moment, it ultimately changed the course of my life for the better.

We all have an internal narrative of how we think life is supposed to go—but it never goes that way. Remember, the flow of life knows what it's doing. The Universe is trying to speak to us and unfold in our favor. One of my favorite quotes is, "God-sent madness is superior to man-made sanity." In other words, the universe always has better plans for us than we could think up on our own.

Always listen to the Universe's nudges and your soul's urge. Even though you don't know how it's going to unfold, trust yourself, trust the Universe, and take action. Don't just stay home and manifest, get out and participate in the world. Give it your best effort, despite not knowing when the returns are going to come and what that's going to look like.

There is no finish line. Life is never going to begin just around the next corner. This moment is now, and now is always life. Learn to enjoy where you are, even as you go for what you want.

CHAPTER TEN

SHOW UP, CELEBRATE, AND BE KIND

We're all hurtling closer to death every moment.

Too morbid? I find it motivating! I want to be at my death and know I earned it, don't you?

So, go for it while you still can. Join the clubs, start the business, make music, go on the trip. Participate in life. We're lucky to be here!

Do what feels right for you. Don't overthink it.

Follow common sense. Stop seeking something outside yourself to make you happy inside.

The only way to ruin your life is to rush around thinking you have a problem to solve. No one is getting out of here alive.

We're all spiritual beings having a human experience, so focus on connecting and creating. Nothing replaces human connection!

When you think of the "good ol' days," remember you still had trials back then. The same holds true today, right here and now. There are always positives as well as lessons to learn. Don't miss your life wishing it was something different—the fact you're even here is an absolute miracle.

Foster an abundance mentality. Other peoples' successes won't keep you from having your own.

Look up. We're on a planet, orbiting a star, hurtling through infinity. No one knows what's going on, and that's okay. Let it be a beautiful mystery. Trust that the Universe always has your back.

Enjoy the incredible gift of being human.

ALWAYS SEND THE TEXT

When I first moved to Austin, I initially signed a fourteen-month lease at a great building, but somewhere in my gut I knew it was a mistake. Just before I moved, I found the perfect spot in the city that came with a nine-month lease. I unwound myself pretty easily from the first one since I hadn't moved in yet and pivoted to the new place.

That lease was up in March 2020—just in time for the pandemic lockdown. Instead of spending money on an apartment far away from my family and friends during that harrowing time, I got to pack up, move home, and be in a pod with all the people I love.

Once I was reinstalled in Salt Lake, I got a call from my old company—I hadn't worked with them for more than two years at this point—asking if I'd do some training for them. In return, they offered to return my sweat equity. I jumped at the chance. Four weeks later, I'd earned two hundred thousand dollars' worth of my business back.

I was already happy that I'd listened to my intuition about the apartment lease in Austin and moving home, but then my niece Brielle was in a serious accident. She has a very steep driveway and was longboarding down it when she fell and hit her head. (Please always wear a helmet, people!) Thankfully, the next-door neighbors were taking a walk, saw her lying unconscious, and called an ambulance.

Without that stroke of luck, Brielle probably would have died there.

She was taken to the hospital, where she stayed in a coma for days. She was connected to machines that kept her alive. A hole was drilled into her skull to decrease the swelling of her brain. We were told the injury she'd sustained was very serious. It wasn't clear whether she was going to live and, if she did, what her capabilities might be.

It was such a traumatic event for our entire family. I was so happy I could be with Brielle and her mother, my sister, Michelle. I felt so overwhelmed and helpless, but at least I was there for support.

Michelle has a big social media following and posted frequent updates about Brielle's condition. At the end of every one, she asked everyone to channel their energy toward healing Brielle. She was like, *I don't care what you believe in—God, Source, Universe—whatever energy you can tap into, please send love.*

A couple of days later, Brielle woke up and started to come back to normal. It was truly a miracle. If you met Brielle today, you would have no idea she'd come that close to dying. She doesn't remember it happening at all.

Recently, I was at Michelle's house for a barbecue. It was

the first time I had a chance to be real with her, one-on-one, since the experience. I asked her, "What's your takeaway from all this?"

She said, "Always send the text. I may not have been able to read everyone's texts at the time, but I know who texted me."

How many times do we think of someone and then decide not to reach out for fear of bothering them? But the thing is, we're all seeking a deeper support system and deeper connection. It's so easy to send a text, and it can make such a difference in someone's life.

These days, anytime I think of someone—whether they're having a birthday, celebration, or traumatic experience—I always send the text. It only takes a few seconds, but now I know how much those few seconds can change the energetic energy around someone else's situation.

STAY PRESENT

A few years back, I was in LA on business and found myself running late one morning. The Uber ride to my meeting was going to take forty minutes in traffic, so I figured I would use that time to knock out a bunch of emails.

Except the Uber driver seemed to have other plans. He was chatting with me nonstop. When he found out I was from

Utah, he wanted to talk about skiing. Living in Park City. How gorgeous the state was.

For the first ten minutes, I kept thinking, *Holy cow, will this guy please shut up. This is so annoying; I have work to do.* Then, I remembered my favorite definition of being mindful is "being completely aware of the present moment without wanting anything to be different."

So, I forced myself to relax. I took a deep breath, released the tension from my shoulders, put my phone down, and gave this guy my full attention. We actually ended up having a great conversation. We joked around about skiing; he gave me some tips and then recommended a few restaurants in Park City he thought I'd like.

At the end of the ride, he turned around and said, "Thank you so much. I'm actually a coder for a living. I work from home and live alone. The reason I drive Uber is not for the money; it's for the human interaction. Our conversation just filled me up for the whole day." I felt great knowing I'd made another person that happy.

This is just another reminder that when we can get out of our heads and become present in the moment, we can always find some magic in our days—and maybe give some of that magic to someone else while we're at it. Practicing mindfulness makes us better people. Try it; you'll like it!

SIT IN THE GOO

As we evolve, grow, "wake up," and realize, *Holy shit, we're alive!*, it's only natural the people we associate with will also tend to shift. We might not jibe with the same people we used to jibe with, and that can feel very scary. Our old friendships may change, and we need to trust that as we level-up in life, new people will come in to support our journey.

This holds especially true during the time when we've grown out of our old network and haven't yet found our new network. But just like the caterpillar doesn't know it's going to turn into a butterfly while it's still a pile of goo in a cocoon, try to remember your struggles will have a beautiful outcome as well. As we level-up in life, we grow and change. Sometimes that means creating new boundaries with people that are holding us back. Our new tribe and new soulmates are going to find us eventually—but we might have to sit in the goo for a little while and wait for them to give us wings.

I went through my transformation pretty quickly, and it caused some tension between me and my two oldest friends, Scott and Nick. Once I realized people learn and grow at different times and the tension only existed because I was trying to force my new beliefs onto them, things got better. You don't have to distance yourself from old friends as long as they support your journey—but you also don't have to shove your latest ideas down their throats.

I'm still close to Scotty to this day, but Nick recently took a time-out on our friendship. Initially, this was absolutely devastating to me. It left me feeling a deep sense of grief.

In the past, I would have tried to "fix" my negative feelings as quickly as I could, which has often led to poor decision-making or saying something defensive I later regret. But this time, I just sat still, got really quiet, and tried to stay aligned. Soon, I realized I was okay with how I was feeling. Emotions are just visitors. They don't stay forever, and the sooner you can accept an emotion, the sooner it will flow through you.

It's only natural to feel sad, grief, and confusion over the loss of a long-term friendship. Once I realized that, I got insights on how I could have been a better friend and how, at times, I may have shown a lack of love in our friendship. Looking back, I realize I've made some mistakes. I see the lesson he's teaching me, and I'm grateful for that. I've left the door open, though, and hope in the future we will find our way back to each other.

We learn by having experiences. This one made me grateful to be open to feeling a wide variety of emotions. It also left me feeling a deep sense of peace and an appreciation for my discomfort.

I thought for a moment my transformation was going to have a negative impact on my relationship with Casey Baugh too, which would have been devastating. Back when Lauren had just broken up with me and I was deeply depressed while selling alarms in Arkansas, I got a phone call from him asking me to come on a road trip.

I eagerly agreed. I had not connected with Casey, one on one, for more than a year at that point. As we drove through the Midwest, he shared that he was concerned about me. He said, "I heard you've been doing drugs, and I just wanted to check in on you." Like I said before, growing up conservative as a Mormon in Utah makes you believe all drugs will kill you—and Casey clearly didn't want me to die.

I took a deep breath and shared everything with him. As soon as I explained my experiences, I could see him relax. He got it. He said, "I know you're going to be okay." He put his arm around me and told me he loved me.

We ended up pulling over and hiking through the woods to a waterfall. Because I had been vulnerable with him, Casey was able to get really vulnerable with me too. He shared with me some questions he had about life as well as several intense situations he'd experienced along the way. It turned out to be one of the most special moments of my life.

My takeaway from it all was: here's this man who is the epitome of success offering me his trust and support, even though everything I was doing went completely against his religious norms. I already knew I was on the right path, but his willingness to stand by me gave me added strength, courage, and confidence. Knowing my mentor was still on my side despite my unconventional journey felt like icing on the cake.

Some of my best friends now are Sam, Kim, Ryan, and Kelsey. We wouldn't have even been friends five years ago because I was in such a different place. Once my frequency and vibe raised to match theirs, along they came into my life, and it has been such a blessing.

The right people will eventually gravitate to us. It doesn't happen overnight, but the Universe is always on time. So, if you're going through an awakening, trust that a new soul tribe will come your way soon enough. Know that the people you love will also get where they need to be eventually, in their own way. It's not your responsibility to do it for them.

Everyone's doing the best that they can. One way isn't better than another way. My journey isn't your journey.

I hope this book provides inspiration for you to dive into your journey with confidence, knowing that the Universe will unfold for you. You have an incredible opportunity to experience an awakening as well, with your own breakthroughs and new perspectives to discover. I encourage you to forge your own path and find the awe and wonder that awaits you.

There's never going to be a time that you're fully "ready." You'll probably be nervous. Take the plunge anyhow. A beautiful life of healing and engagement is there for you if you're willing to do the work.

This is your invitation to start unlocking the mysteries that make you, *you*. Your story will undoubtedly be just as exciting as mine has been. I'm here to cheer you on, and if you ever need support reach out to me @doug_cartwright on Facebook, Twitter, and Instagram. I answer every DM!

TEN TIPS FOR LIFE ON EARTH

Here are a few more truth bombs I want to lob at you before we wrap things up. This list is pretty much a crystallization of everything I've told you throughout this book and serves as a quick and dirty reference if you're ever feeling lost. Post it somewhere you can easily see it, check it out whenever you need to, and start incorporating these lessons into your everyday life wherever you can.

1. **Be human.** Sleep, hydrate, get outside, laugh, jump in the ocean, sing in the kitchen, say, "I love you," and be playful.
2. **Trust the flow.** The Universe knows what it's doing, so

let it happen. Our atmosphere blocks deadly solar rays. Our life is dependent on a massive burning hydrogen ball in the sky that gives us light. Our most important resource for life falls from the sky. You can definitely trust what's going on here.

3. **Sit still.** *Silence your mind, and your soul will speak.* Allow the answers to come. Follow your nudges. Listen to the whispers. Eliminate noise, so you can tap back into yourself.

4. **Stay curious.** Ask questions. It's okay to say, "I don't know." Wonder why things work. Pretend you're looking at everything for the first time. How would an intelligent species from another planet look at our world if they just landed here? Act like you have a new set of eyes and start seeing things with awe and wonder again.

5. **Be nice.** Everyone is fighting a battle, so be nice. Help others, and lessen their suffering. Be a good human.

6. **Participate.** Go to the event, join the new club, buy the plane ticket, show up for others. Always say yes to new experiences.

7. **Celebrate.** Be happy for other people's wins. Get on social media for thirty minutes every day to like people's pictures and respond to their stories. Tell them, "That's awesome" or "Good job!" Ninety-nine percent of people are posting on social media for validation, so give it to them. Validating other people doesn't take anything away from you. Be the ultimate hype friend. Eat the cake; jump up and down when you get good news; celebrate your life and the lives of those around you.

8. **Create.** Share your talents. Make art and music. Dance. Have sex. Don't be intimidated to share your creations. You have specific, unique talents that no one else has. Whether you create a business or art or music or a family, creation is creation. Let everyone see what you're up to!

9. **Stay open.** Connect with those around you. Look at strangers; make eye contact; open your heart; be vulnerable; speak freely. Have a genuine interest in others. Always stay open to the synchronicities of the Universe.

10. **Look up.** Ponder your existence in this vast universe. Every star you see could have another planet just like Earth. Feel the cosmic perspective.

All of these things embody the feeling and meaning of the *holy shit, we're alive* experience—and now you know what to do next.

CONCLUSION

So, there you have it: my not quite memoir, sort of self-help book. Here's hoping my journey offers you some new insights, makes you curious to try new things, and inspires you to make positive changes in your life. Mostly, though, I hope it makes you feel less alone in our shared humanity.

But in case you ever need reminding, being human is an incredible gift. The fact that we even get to be here at all is a miracle. The next time you look up into the night sky, remember that we're just a tiny speck floating in an infinite cosmic ocean.

As scientist Carl Sagan said after the earth appeared as a pale blue dot roughly 3.7 billion miles away when NASA's Voyager One took a picture of us right before it left our solar system:

Consider again that dot. That's here. That's home. That's us. On it everyone you love, everyone you know, everyone you ever heard of, every human being who ever was, lived out their lives... There is perhaps no better demonstration of the folly of human conceits than this distant image of our tiny world. To me, it underscores our responsibility to deal more kindly with one another and to preserve and cherish the pale blue dot, the only home we've ever known.

Recognizing our place in the universe, on this little fraction of a pixel in the middle of nowhere, can help us let go of what we thought life was supposed to be. It can help us move past the stories that are holding us back and trust that something bigger has our best intentions in mind, so we can finally enjoy being inside our own heads. We can love being ourselves. We can live an enriching life full of enthusiasm, excitement, love, and joy. We can rest assured that life is happening for us, not to us.

Because we aren't just here in the universe—we actually *are* the universe. We're the universe experiencing ourselves. The same atoms in the supernova that created life are what make up our bones and bodies. Let's all celebrate the opportunity to be a part of this grand cosmic adventure because it's the adventure of a lifetime with endless possibilities.

Appreciate the life you're actually living right now, not the one you're trying to make happen or the one you wish was happening. Don't miss the beautiful moments appearing in front of you even as you read this. Become the person that if everyone acted the same way, there would be world peace, love, and connection.

Do things that make you feel alive. When you feel alive, you're open to inspiration—and inspiration is what will change the world. Change your story; find the flow; maximize your human experience.

Holy shit, we're alive!

Doug

Want to know more and go even deeper? You can find me on The Daily Shifts app, at www.thedailyshifts.com, and @doug_cartwright on Facebook, Twitter, and Instagram. I offer a variety of tools, guided meditations, courses, e-books, workbooks, masterclasses, training groups, and coaching programs full of cool people just like you who are looking for something more out of life. I respond to every single DM, so don't be afraid to reach out. It would be my honor to get to know and work with you.